CRIM MOVIE QUIZ BOOK

JAY ROBERT NASH

Chicago Review Press
213 West Institute Place • Chicago, Illinois 60610

This book is for P. Michael O'Sullivan

Crime Movie Quiz Book
Copyright © 1983 by Jay Robert Nash
All right reserved. Printed in the United States of America

Library of Congress Catalog Card Number 82-60659

ISBN   0-914091-30-1   Paperbound

Published by Chicago Review Press
213 West Institute Place
Chicago, Illinois 60610

Cover design by Cathy Anetsberger

Contents

The Other Side of the Curtain   1

The P.I.s   3

Gangsters & Gun Molls   21

The Long Arm   39

Bad Women   54

Gunmen & Peacemakers   68

Behind the Gray Walls   83

Murder Most Foul and Otherwise   99

Inside the Outfit   118

The Caper   132

Miscellaneous Miscreants   146

Solutions   163

THE OTHER SIDE OF THE CURTAIN

Whether they be gangster epics or murder mysteries, cop films or prison pictures, crime movies have an abiding fascination for the viewing public. The fans and buffs of such movies are legion and it is for this devoted (and relentless) audience that *Crime Movie Quiz Book* was created.

The quizzes herein cover the entire spectrum of crime movies, including the killers, outlaws, private detectives, the great caper flicks and the whodunits, with quizzes geared to test the most astute aficionado of *film noir*. The quizzes will challenge the reader and will—it's hoped—spark recall of the hot, bright images that crime films, from the silents to the present, have implanted within the public's memory. All of it, the author believes, will provide great fun.

Armchair detectives, amateur sleuths and movie trivia buffs should do well with these quizzes, particularly those fans who are addicted to the late show on TV. The student of the genre will undoubtedly do exceptionally well, that is, if he or she knows his hoods, goons, wardens, convicts, homicidal maniacs, gumshoes, flatfoots, boxmen, outlaws, and just plain bad women, about 75 years of those who have lived, as Blasco Ibanez said in *Blood and Sand,* "on the other side of the curtain."

1

Those averaging 50 percent correct answers per quiz should think themselves fairly well versed in *film noir*. Readers scoring 75 percent are super sleuths who can justly walk beside Basil Rathbone and Nigel Bruce through Limehouse at midnight. Anyone answering 90 percent of the quizzes correctly should be making his own crime movies a la Mr. Huston and Mr. Hawks.

Sharpen your memory, and good luck.

How to Reach a Verdict

There are two ways to score your answers in the *Crime Movie Quiz Book*. Each chapter is made up of a group of quizzes, A through E (with one quiz F in the last group of quizzes), with the more difficult quizzes given a higher point score. As you finish each chapter, you can rate your expertise by checking the solutions (starting on page 163) and totaling your point scores to see just how well you know each area of crime movies. At the end of the book, total your points from all the chapters and rate yourself against the crime movie masters.

THE P.I.s

The private detective in movies is a creature of many moods and manners. He is, like the immortal Sherlock Holmes, probably the most played (but never played-out) gumshoe in the films, a noble and virtuous character, not only seeking the solution to a crime but insisting that truth and justice be equally served. Joining the master Holmes are such super sleuths as the sophisticated Philo Vance, the indefatigable Bulldog Drummond, the whimsical but always perceptive Nick Charles.

On the other side of the coin we have the tough but clever ones—Sam Spade, Philip Marlowe, and Mike Hammer. In the end, they too solve the crimes that baffle the police departments of the world, not with Holmes' wry smile, but with bloody knuckles. These are tough boys, but honest, serving either the public good or the worth of their own off-beat codes.

In films, the private eye has always held a special attraction for viewing audiences, for his is the position of man-against-the-underworld, with the underworld invariably getting the worst of it. Of course it was the Bogarts and Rathbones that made the memorable detectives of fiction come alive, along with a host of other suave or two-fisted stars, including some wonderful ladies young and old, screen personalities who stalked evil nervelessly, their purpose clear, their pursuit relentless.

The following quizzes test your recall of the screen's greatest private eyes.

QUIZ A

Score 5 points for each correct answer.

1. Match the silent era actors with the silent films in which they played the immortal Sherlock Holmes.

_____ **1.** Maurice Costello

_____ **2.** Harry Benham

_____ **3.** James Bragington

_____ **4.** William Gillette

_____ **5.** John Barrymore

A. *Sherlock Holmes (1916)*

B. *Adventures of Sherlock Holmes (1903)*

C. *The Sign of Four (1913)*

D. *Sherlock Holmes (1922)*

E. *A Study in Scarlet (1914)*

2. Match the actor to the talking Sherlock.

_____ **1.** Clive Brook

_____ **2.** Raymond Massey

_____ **3.** Basil Rathbone

_____ **4.** Robert Stephens

_____ **5.** Nicol Williamson

A. *The Speckled Band (1931)*

B. *The Hound of the Baskervilles (1939)*

C. *The Seven Percent Solution (1976)*

D. *The Return of Sherlock Holmes (1929)*

E. *The Private Life of Sherlock Holmes (1970)*

3. Match the actor who played Professor Moriarity in the following Holmes epics.

_____ **1.** Gustav von Seffertitz

_____ **2.** George Zucco

_____ **3.** Ernest Torrence

_____ **4.** Lionel Atwill

_____ **5.** Henry Daniel

_____ **6.** Lyn Harding

_____ **7.** Harry T. Morey

A. *The Woman in Green* (1945)

B. *Sherlock Holmes* (1922)

C. *Sherlock Holmes* (1932)

D. *The Triumph of Sherlock Holmes* (U.K., 1935)

E. *Sherlock Holmes and the Secret Weapon* (1942)

F. *The Return of Sherlock Holmes* (1929)

G. *Adventures of Sherlock Holmes* (1939)

4. Match the film detective to the actor who portrayed him.

_____ **1.** Sam Spade

_____ **2.** Philip Marlowe

_____ **3.** Hercule Poirot

_____ **4.** Peter Wimsey

_____ **5.** Charlie Chan

_____ **6.** Nick Charles

_____ **7.** Perry Mason

A. Albert Finney in *Murder on the Orient Express*

B. Sidney Toler in *Sky Dragon*

C. Warren William in *The Case of the Velvet Claws*

D. William Powell in

_____ **8.** Simon Templar   *The Thin Man*

_____ **9.** Slim Callaghan

_____ **10.** Nero Wolfe

E. Michael Rennie in *Uneasy Terms* (U.K. 1948)

F. Robert Montgomery in *Busman's Honeymoon*

G. George Sanders in *The Saint Takes Over*

H. Walter Connolly in *The League of Missing Men*

I. Humphrey Bogart in *The Maltese Falcon*

J. Dick Powell in *Murder My Sweet*

5. Match the actor to film in which he played sleuth Philo Vance.

_____ **1.** William Powell

_____ **2.** Basil Rathbone

_____ **3.** Warren William

_____ **4.** Paul Lukas

_____ **5.** Edmund Lowe

_____ **6.** Wilfred Hyde White

_____ **7.** Grant Richards

_____ **8.** Alan Curtis

A. *The Garden Murder Case*

B. *The Scarab Murder Case*

C. *Philo Vance's Gamble*

D. *The Bishop Murder Case*

E. *The Canary Murder Case*

_____ **9.** William Wright   **F.** *Calling Philo Vance*

_____ **10.** James Stephenson   **G.** *The Casino Murder Case*

H. *Philo Vance Returns*

I. *Night of Mystery*

J. *The Dragon Murder Case*

6. Match the Actor to the movie in which he played the brutal private eye, Mike Hammer.

_____ **1.** Biff Elliott   **A.** *The Girl Hunters*

_____ **2.** Ralph Meeker   **B.** *My Gun Is Quick*

_____ **3.** Mickey Spillane   **C.** *I, The Jury*

_____ **4.** Robert Bray   **D.** *Kiss Me Deadly*

7. Match the actor to the Bulldog Drummond film in which he played the title role.

_____ **1.** Ralph Richardson   **A.** *Bulldog Drummond Strikes Back*

_____ **2.** Ronald Coleman

_____ **3.** John Howard   **B.** *Bulldog Drummond's Revenge*

_____ **4.** Ray Milland

_____ **5.** Walter Pidgeon   **C.** *Bulldog Drummond Escapes*

D. *Calling Bulldog Drummond*

E. *Return of Bulldog Drummond*

8. Match the habits of the detective to the actor and film.

_____ **1.** Cultivated rare flowers   **A.** Nicol Williamson in *The Seven Percent Solution*

_____ **2.** Was addicted to drugs

_____ **3.** Was addicted to alcohol

_____ **4.** Raised tropical fish

_____ **5.** Was addicted to cigars

B. William Powell in *The Thin Man*

C. Edward Arnold in *Meet Nero Wolfe*

D. Lloyd Nolan in *Michael Shayne, Private Detective*

E. Warren William in *The Lone Wolf Strikes*

9. Match the detective's side-kick with the actor who portrayed him.

_____ **1.** Runt in Boston Blackie films

_____ **2.** Birmingham Brown in Charlie Chan films

_____ **3.** Archie in *Meet Nero Wolfe*

_____ **4.** Goldy in *The Falcon Takes Over*

_____ **5.** Algy in *Bulldog Drummond Strikes Back*

A. Mantan Moreland

B. George E. Stone

C. Charles Butterworth

D. Lionel Stander

E. Allen Jenkins

10. Match the private eye with his girlfriend.

_____ **1.** *Klute*

_____ **2.** *Harper*

_____ **3.** J.J. Gittes in *Chinatown*

_____ **4.** *McQ*

_____ **5.** Philip Marlowe in *Lady in the Lake*

A. An incestuous heiress

B. An editor

C. A call girl

D. His estranged wife

E. A female informer

QUIZ B

The following statements are either true or false. Score 3 points for each correct answer.

1. Margaret Rutherford played Agatha Christie's Miss Marple in *Murder Most Foul*. True or False?

2. Ellery Queen in the 1935 movie *The Spanish Cape Mystery* was portrayed by Ralph Bellamy. True or False?

3. Donald Woods played Perry Mason in the film *The Case of the Lucky Legs*. True or False?

4. The gunsel Wilmer in *The Maltese Falcon* was portrayed by Elisha Cook, Jr. True or False?

5. Tom Conway played the lead role in all the Falcon movies. True or False?

6. Paul Newman's role in *The Drowning Pool* was based upon Ross McDonald's detective Lew Archer. True or False?

7. Jacques Tourneur directed *Nick Carter, Master Detective* in 1939. True or False?

8. Nancy Drew was played in various films by Bonita Granville, Judy Garland and Googie Withers. True or False?

9. *Murder She Said* was the first film in which Margaret Rutherford appeared as Miss Marple. True or False?

10. All films and TV series based on Dick Tracy starred either Ralph Byrd or Morgan Conway. True or False?

QUIZ C

Score 4 points for each correct answer.

1. The last word(s) uttered in *The Maltese Falcon* (1941) was(were)

_____ **A.** "I'm sending you over."

_____ **B.** "Huh?"

_____ **C.** "This is the stuff dreams are made of."

2. Sam Spade in the movies was played by

_____ **A.** Humphrey Bogart.

_____ **B.** Warren William.

_____ **C.** Ricardo Cortez.

_____ **D.** All of the above.

3. The 1941 production of *The Maltese Falcon* was directed by

_____ **A.** Raoul Walsh.

_____ **B.** John Huston.

_____ **C.** Michael Curtiz.

4. The clue to a murderer's identity in *The Dark Corner* is

_____ **A.** an off-brand of cigars.

_____ **B.** an unusual shoe print.

_____ **C.** a laundry mark.

5. Albert Finney played detective Eddie Ginley in

_____ **A.** *Shamus.*

_____ **B.** *Gumshoe.*

_____ **C.** *Flatfoot.*

6. Richard Roundtree played P.I. John Shaft in which of following films?

_____ **A.** *Shaft*

_____ **B.** *Shaft's Big Score*

_____ **C.** *Shaft in Africa*

_____ **D.** All of the above

7. Nick Charles' wife Nora was portrayed in all the Thin Man films by

_____ **A.** Greer Garson.

_____ **B.** Lupe Velez.

_____ **C.** Myrna Loy.

8. Who sets up his own murder in a film that led to an off-beat movie series featuring an equally off-beat detective?

_____ **A.** Melvyn Douglas in *Arsene Lupin Returns*

_____ **B.** Melvyn Douglas in *The Lone Wolf Returns*

_____ **C.** Richard Dix in *The Whistler*

9. Which of the following books by Raymond Chandler were made into films?

_____ **A.** *The Little Sister*

_____ **B.** *Trouble is My Business*

_____ **C.** *The Big Sleep*

_____ **D.** All of the above

10. Professor Moriarity, in *The Adventures of Sherlock Holmes,* attempts to

_____ **A.** steal the crown jewels of England.

_____ **B.** murder Queen Victoria.

_____ **C.** set fire to the British Museum.

QUIZ D

Use your deductive reasoning, the process of elimination, and your "hunches" to match the film detective with his peronality and historical profile. Score 5 points for each correct answer.

1. Philip Marlowe

2. Philo Vance

3. Bulldog Drummond

4. Sam Spade

5. Ellery Queen

_____ **A.** There are three major films based on this hard-boiled San Francisco private eye whose partner, portrayed in one version by Jerome Cowan, is mysteriously shot and killed in the first reel. The P.I. embarks on a quest for the killer, and, in the process, stumbles upon a piece of antiquity allegedly worth a fortune.

_____ **B.** He is a dilettante and an aesthete who is expert in the fields of arts, music, philosophy and religion, applying his knowledge in these areas to solve murders. There were 15 major films produced between 1929 and 1947 based on this sophisticated sleuth.

_____ **C.** A British ex-captain who, after being mustered out of the army following World War I (this theme dropped in later films), he patriotically pursues Britain's enemies, his chief nemesis being the arch-villain Carl Peterson, portrayed by Montagu Love in a 1929 film on this dogged detective.

_____ **D.** He is a sometime writer and a collector of rare books who helps his father, a police inspector, solve seemingly impossible murders, mostly through his powers of observation a la Holmes. Films about this brash young detective appeared from 1935 to 1972.

_____ **E.** A tough, wise-cracking Los Angeles private eye, he solves his cases but is never a personal winner. His creator, born in Chicago, was of great writing talent. Films from 1944 to 1975 established this anti-social loser as a classic private eye.

QUIZ E

Name the classic detective movies from which scenes are shown on the next few pages. Score 5 points for each correct answer.

1. Humphrey Bogart, Peter Lorre, Mary Astor and Sydney Greenstreet only have eyes for the curious item in Bogart's hands in this 1941 film entitled:

2. Peter Lorre, who played this inscrutable oriental sleuth
in a number of films, gets the drop on the villains in:

3. This scatterbrained radio comedienne, shown surrounded by intimidating cops, had a 1939 Paramount film, dealing with detective Philo Vance, named after her. It was called:

4. Sidney Toler and Victor Sen Yung try to solve the mysterious death of an author on board the *China Clipper* in:

5. Sterling Hayden, Elliott Gould, and Nina Van Pallandt on the beach at Malibu in the 1973 United Artists production of:

Scoring

Quiz A _____

Quiz B _____

Quiz C _____

Quiz D _____

Quiz E _____

Chapter Total Score _____

Your Super Sleuth Rating

If you scored between 425 and 383   You're entitled to your own private eye office *with* secretary.

If you scored between 382 and 319   You're capable of tracking any shifty-eyed miscreant.

If you scored between 318 and 212   You need more than a magnifying glass to follow the trail.

GANGSTERS & GUN MOLLS

Gangsters have elbowed and shoved their way across the screens since the silent cinema went to three reels. No other genre was as closely and hotly recorded by the motion picture industry as the gangster. In fact, in the early 1930s real events and personalities were put into major films only months after they made the headlines and in this way the films presented a living chronicle of America's underworld in all its posturing bravado and thin glamour.

With the advent of sound, the most impactful films were those in which a new breed of film stars appeared, snarling snapping and bantering types such as James Cagney, Humphrey Bogart, and Edward G. Robinson ("The Big Three") who were all, not so ironically, Warner Brothers contract players. So popular did this genre in crime become that even sophisticated actors like Robert Montgomery and Edmund Lowe turned for a time to the portrayal of illiterate thugs who made their way up the ladder of success with machine-gun in hand, dealing with rivals by "bumping them off," "taking them for a ride" and "fixing their wagon." An entire new lexicon came into being through the gangster epics where cops were "bulls," informers were "squealers," where to escape was to "take it on the lam," and to die in gangster gunfire was to "croak" or "cash in." It is as dead a language today as Latin Vulgate.

21

QUIZ A

Score 5 points for each correct answer.

1. Match the actor who played the real-life gangster.

_____	**1.** Charles Bronson	**A.** *The Rise and Fall of Legs Diamond*
_____	**2.** Lawrence Tierney	
_____	**3.** Ray Danton	**B.** *Al Capone*
_____	**4.** Rod Steiger	**C.** *Love Me or Leave Me* (Martin "The Gimp" Snyder)
_____	**5.** David Jansen	
_____	**6.** Vic Morrow	**D.** *The St. Valentine's Day Massacre* (Capone)
_____	**7.** Nick Adams	
_____	**8.** Mickey Rooney	**E.** *Young Dillinger*
_____	**9.** James Cagney	**F.** *Dillinger*
_____	**10.** Ralph Meeker	**G.** *Machine Gun Kelly*
		H. *King of the Roaring Twenties* (Arnold Rothstein)
		I. *Portrait of A Mobster* (Dutch Schultz)
		J. *Baby Face Nelson*

2. Match the film gangster to the actor and the motion picture in which he appeared.

_____	**1.** Trigger	**A.** Douglas Fairbanks, Jr., in *Little Caesar*
_____	**2.** Duke Mantee	
_____	**3.** Tony Camonte	**B.** George Bancroft in *Underworld*
_____	**4.** Mileway Barry	

_____ **5.** Joe Massara

_____ **6.** Lou "Legs" Ricarno

_____ **7.** Bull Weed

_____ **8.** Nick Scarsi

_____ **9.** Louis Scorpio

_____ **10.** Louis Blanco

C. Wallace Beery in *The Secret Six*

D. Clark Gable in *The Finger Points*

E. Humphrey Bogart in *The Petrified Forest*

F. Jack LaRue in *The Story of Temple Drake*

G. Paul Muni in *Scarface*

H. Louis Wolheim in *The Racket*

I. Lew Ayres in *Doorway to Hell*

J. Edmund Lowe in *Dressed to Kill* (1928)

3. Match the gun moll to the female star who played her in films.

_____ **1.** Feathers McCoy

_____ **2.** Gaye Dawn

_____ **3.** Marie Garson

_____ **4.** Doll Conovan

_____ **5.** Blondie

_____ **6.** Tootsie Malone

_____ **7.** Gwen Allen

_____ **8.** Poppy

_____ **9.** Debby Marsh

_____ **10.** Jean Morgan

A. Gloria Grahame in *The Big Heat*

B. Jean Hagen in *The Asphalt Jungle*

C. Temple Texas in *The Kiss of Death*

D. Muriel Evans in *Manhattan Melodrama*

E. Jean Harlow in *The Public Enemy*

F. Ann Dvorak in
G-Men

G. Karen Morley in
Scarface

H. Evelyn Brent in
Underworld

I. Ida Lupino in
High Sierra

J. Claire Trevor in
Key Largo

4. Match the movie to the actor who played Al Capone.

_____ **1.** Louis Wolheim	**A.**	*Capone*
_____ **2.** Wallace Beery	**B.**	*Al Capone*
_____ **3.** Paul Muni	**C.**	*The Scarface Mob*
_____ **4.** Edward G. Robinson	**D.**	*The Finger Points*
_____ **5.** Lee J. Cobb	**E.**	*The Secret Six*
_____ **6.** Clark Gable	**F.**	*Little Caesar*
_____ **7.** Rod Steiger	**G.**	*The St. Valentine's Day Massacre*
_____ **8.** Jason Robards, Jr.		
_____ **9.** Ben Gazzara	**H.**	*Party Girl*
_____ **10.** Neville Brand	**I.**	*Scarface*
	J.	*The Racket*

5. Match the actor who played the side-kick to the gangster.

_____ **1.** Clark Gable in *Manhattan Melodrama*

_____ **2.** Humphrey Bogart in *Dead End*

_____ **3.** James Cagney in *The Roaring Twenties*

A. Van Heflin

B. Frank McHugh

C. Nat Pendleton

D. Maxie Rosenbloom

E. Allen Jenkins

_____ **4.** Robert Taylor in
Johnny Eager

_____ **5.** Edward G. Robinson
in *The Amazing Dr.
Clitterhouse*

6. Match the actor and the movie to the memorable
gangster line.

_____ **1.** "Take him for a
ride."

_____ **2.** "I gotta teach a guy
a lesson."

_____ **3.** "Get out my way—
I'm spittin'!"

_____ **4.** "Get back or I'll give
it to him right in the
head!"

_____ **5.** "Don't bone me!"

A. Dwight Frye in
Doorway to Hell

B. Paul Muni in
Scarface

C. Wheeler Oakman
in *Lights of New
York*

D. Sterling Hayden in
The Asphalt Jungle

E. James Cagney in
*Angels with Dirty
Faces*

7. Match the actor and film to the gangster's dying words.

_____ **1.** "Made it, Ma! Top of
the World!"

_____ **2.** "Mother of Mercy—
is this the end of
Rico?"

_____ **3.** "Get back,—
I'm going out!"

_____ **4.** "Marie! Marie!"

_____ **5.** "If pa just hangs on
to that black colt,
everything's gonna
be okay."

A. Edward G.
Robinson in *Little
Caesar*

B. Sterling Hayden in
The Asphalt Jungle

C. James Cagney in
White Heat

D. Humphrey Bogart
in *Dead End*

E. Humphrey Bogart
in *High Sierra*

8. Match the director to his classic gangster film.

_____ **1.** *Scarface*
_____ **2.** *White Heat*
_____ **3.** *The Musketeers of Pig Alley*
_____ **4.** *Manhattan Melodrama*
_____ **5.** *Dead End*

A. Raoul Walsh
B. D.W. Griffith
C. W.S. Van Dyke, II
D. Howard Hawks
E. William Wyler

9. Match the gangster George Raft played to the movie in which he appeared.

_____ **1.** *Each Dawn I Die*
_____ **2.** *Invisible Stripes*
_____ **3.** *Scarface*
_____ **4.** *Quick Millions*
_____ **5.** *Some Like It Hot*

A. Gino Rinaldi
B. Spats Colombo
C. Jimmy Kirk
D. Cliff Taylor
E. "Hood" Stacey

10. Match the gangster Humphrey Bogart played to the movie in which he appeared.

_____ **1.** *Bullets or Ballots*
_____ **2.** *Kid Galahad*
_____ **3.** *Brother Orchid*
_____ **4.** *King of the Underworld*
_____ **5.** *The Big Shot*

A. Joe Gurney
B. Bugs Fenner
C. Jack Buck
D. Duke Berne
E. Turkey Morgan

QUIZ B

The following statements are either true or false.

Score 3 points for each correct answer.

1. Trock Estrella, the gangster who terrorized the neighborhood in *Winterset* was played by Ted DeCorsia. True or False?

2. The gangster who terrorized fishermen in *Out of the Fog* was played by John Garfield. True or False?

3. The plastic surgery performed on Bruce Cabot's face in *Let 'Em Have It* was purposely botched by the doctor who intended to scar the gangster for life. True or False?

4. In *Angel on My Shoulder*, Paul Muni plays the role of a gangster from hell who takes over the body of an ethical politician. True or False?

5. In the *Earl of Chicago*, Robert Montgomery is a British nobleman who turns to crime. True or False?

6. One of George Raft's most memorable speeches was uttered in *Hell on Frisco Bay* about a rival gangster: "Big Ed, great big Ed. You know why they call him Big Ed? Because he's got big ideas. Some day he's gonna get a big idea about me—and it's gonna be his last!" True or False?

7. John Ford's gangster comedy, *The Whole Town's Talking*, had Edward G. Robinson playing dual roles. True or False?

8. Humphrey Bogart starred in *The Last Gangster*. True or False?

9. Humphrey Bogart played the role of the aging gangster Roy Earle in *High Sierra*. True of False?

10. Lloyd Nolan played the gang boss in *Johnny Apollo*. True or False?

QUIZ C

Score 4 points for each correct answer.

1. Which was the first gangster film?

_____ **A.** *Musketeers of Pig Alley.*

_____ **B.** *Up The River*

_____ **C.** *Broadway*

2. In which film did a gangster first flip a coin?

_____ **A.** *Scarface*

_____ **B.** *Doorway to Hell*

_____ **C.** *Public Enemy*

3. Which film was the first to show gangsters using machine-guns?

_____ **A.** *Blondie Johnson*

_____ **B.** *Gangs of New York*

_____ **C.** *Underworld*

4. The gangland Boss hunting Jack Lemmon and Tony Curtis in *Some Like It Hot* was portrayed by

_____ **A.** Moroni Olson.

_____ **B.** George Raft.

_____ **C.** Edward G. Robinson.

5. Edward G. Robinson, threatening to take action against a rival gangster in *Little Caesar*, snarls:

_____ **A.** "I'm gonna let my piece [gun] speak for me!"

_____ **B.** "He's gonna know who runs this burg!"

_____ **C.** "I'll knock that bozo over before midnight."

6. James Cagney, emgerging from a rival gangster's headquarters, critically wounded after a shoot-out, falls to his knees in a gutter, drenched by rain, in *Public Enemy*, and states:

_____ **A.** "I showed 'em my metal all right!"

_____ **B.** "Those rats won't squeal no more!"

_____ **C.** "I ain't so tough!"

7. The role of Googie, a gangster in *City for Conquest*, was played by

_____ **A.** Barton MacLane.

_____ **B.** Frank McHugh.

_____ **C.** Elia Kazan.

8. The lead role in *Roger Touhy, Gangster*, was enacted by

_____ **A.** Preston Foster.

_____ **B.** Robert Preston.

_____ **C.** Victor McLaughlin.

9. In *Scarface*, George Raft developed a film trademark by flipping a coin. It was

_____ **A.** a half dollar.

_____ **B.** a quarter.

_____ **C.** a nickel.

10. The role of Tony Mako in *Four Hours To Kill* was played by

_____ **A.** Clive Brook.

_____ **B.** Colin Clive.

_____ **C.** Richard Barthlemess.

QUIZ D

Match the film gangster with his profile. Score 5 points for each correct answer.

1. Rocky Sullivan

2. Rocks Valentine

3. Baby Face Martin

4. Little John Sarto

5. "Bugs" Raymond

_____ **A.** A big-time racketeer, this gangster realizes that his days are numbered so he retires, going to Europe. Upon his return five years later, the big shot attempts to resume his role as crime czar only to be attacked by his former henchmen. He seeks refuge in a remote monastery and there finds peace tending flowers. He returns to the city as a monk and, mustering the forces of good, runs his one-time friends, the hoodlums, out of a protection racket.

_____ **B.** He is a truck driver with ambition who goes into racketeering, organizing drivers and then demanding protection money. The gangster rises to great power and plans on marrying into society but his chosen one is in love with another. He plans to kidnap the woman but his own "torpedoes" take him for a one-way ride.

_____ **C.** A one-time slum kid who has robbed his way through life and spent most of his youth in reform school, this tough becomes a prominent gangster who returns after doing a "stretch" in prison to find his former partners have grabbed off his business interests which he promptly takes back. His boyhood friend, a local priest, begins a campaign against him. The gangster shoots his partners when they double-cross him and this leads to a wild shoot-out with police, brought to a halt by the appearance of the priest.

_____ **D.** He is a hardened thief who heads a gang of happy-go-lucky heisters until the mob is taken over by a criminologist studying the behavior of miscreants. He attempts to kill the criminologist by locking him in a cold storage vault after a fur robbery but fails, and, in turn, is murdered by the crime-studying doctor who slips him a poisoned highball.

_____ **E.** Near the top of the public enemy list, this gangster is sought everywhere for bank robbery but he returns to his old neighborhood on the Lower East side of New York to see his mother, who rejects him and his girlfriend who has become a prostitute. Taking revenge on his fate, the gangster attempts a kidnapping and is shot by a resident of the neighborhood.

QUIZ E

Name the classic gangster films from which scenes are shown on the following pages. Score 5 points for each correct answer.

1. George Bancroft as Bull Weed is shown here planning his escape from prison in:

2. Paul Muni, flanked by Karen Moreley and Vince Barnet, is about to test a "chopper" in:

3. Gun-toting gangster James Cagney, as Tom Powers, contemplates his future as his moll, portrayed by sultry Jean Harlow, looks on in:

4. Edward G. Robinson thinks his friend is about to squeal
to the cops in:

5. Humphrey Bogart is stymied by Edward G. Robinson's automatic in:

Scoring

Quiz A   _____

Quiz B   _____

Quiz C   _____

Quiz D   _____

Quiz E   _____

Chapter Total Score   _____

Your Criminologist Rating

If you scored between 470 and 423 You are top expert on the world of the gangster.

If you scored between 422 and 352 You know all "the boys," if not Mr. Big!

If you scored between 351 and 325 Don't put on any double-breasted pin striped suits.

THE LONG ARM

Law enforcement officers have traditionally been shown in motion pictures as bumbling awkward creatures, from Keystone Cops day to a decade or so ago when Hollywood began to treat them as tough and clever people equal to the cunning of their criminal adversaries. There have been notable exceptions such as McPherson in *Laura* and McLeod in *Detective Story*.

In the 1920s and 1930s, the reader should recall, the uniformed cop or the plainclothes police detective was, by and large, frozen in the mold of the thick-headed flatfoot who served as comic relief in the private detective genre. Since that time the movie cop has grown up from wise-cracking bumbler to intelligent and indefatigable sleuth.

Here then are quizzes designed to test your knowledge of the movie cops as well as your memory of some of Hollywood's most unforgettable crime movies where the police detective actually solved the crime.

QUIZ A

Score 5 points for each correct answer.

1. Match the movie to the actor who portrayed the cop.

_____	**1.** Clint Eastwood	**A.**	*Walking Tall*
_____	**2.** Dana Andrews	**B.**	*Bullitt*
_____	**3.** Steve McQueen	**C.**	*Detective Story*
_____	**4.** Richard Widmark	**D.**	*The Detective*
_____	**5.** Joe Don Baker	**E.**	*Laura*
_____	**6.** Charles Laughton	**F.**	*The Killers*
_____	**7.** Kirk Douglas	**G.**	*This Gun for Hire*
_____	**8.** Edmund O'Brien	**H.**	*Madigan*
_____	**9.** Frank Sinatra	**I.**	*Dirty Harry*
_____	**10.** Robert Preston	**J.**	*The Man on the Eiffel Tower*

2. Match the actor to the movie in which he played a federal law enforcement officer.

_____	**1.** Richard Arlen	**A.**	*North by Northwest*
_____	**2.** Robert Preston	**B.**	*G-Men*
_____	**3.** James Cagney	**C.**	*White Heat*
_____	**4.** John Wayne	**D.**	*Johnny Allegro*
_____	**5.** Leo G. Carroll	**E.**	*The F.B.I. Story*
_____	**6.** John Archer	**F.**	*Parole Fixer*
_____	**7.** Dick Powell	**G.**	*Let 'Em Have It*
_____	**8.** James Stewart	**H.**	*Illegal Traffic*
_____	**9.** Jack Carson	**I.**	*The Tall Target*
_____	**10.** George Raft	**J.**	*Big Jim McClain*

3. Match the movie to the actor who played the under-cover federal agent.

_____   **1.** Humphrey Bogart   **A.** *T-Men*

_____   **2.** Cary Grant   **B.** *White Heat*

_____   **3.** Edmund O'Brien   **C.** *Border Incident*

_____   **4.** Edward G. Robinson   **D.** *Background to Danger*

_____   **5.** James Cagney

_____   **6.** Robert Taylor   **E.** *This Is My Affair*

_____   **7.** William Ethe   **F.** *The House on 92nd Street*

_____   **8.** Dennis O'Keefe   **G.** *Across the Pacific*

_____   **9.** George Murphy   **H.** *The Stranger*

_____   **10.** George Raft   **I.** *Notorious*

                                       J. *13 Rue Madelaine*

4. Match the actors to the movies in which they played district attorneys.

_____   **1.** Humphrey Bogart   **A.** *The District Attorney*

_____   **2.** Brian Donlevy

_____   **3.** Henry Morgan   **B.** *The Maltese Falcon*

_____   **4.** Adolphe Menjou   **C.** *A Place in the Sun*

_____   **5.** John Hamilton   **D.** *They Won't Forget*

_____   **6.** Kent Smith   **E.** *The Postman Always Rings Twice* (1946)

_____   **7.** Leon Ames

_____   **8.** Claude Rains   **F.** *Manhattan Melodrama*

_____   **9.** Raymond Burr   **G.** *Party Girl*

_____   **10.** William Powell   **H.** *Murder, Inc.*

                                       I. *Kiss of Death*

                                       J. *The Enforcer* (1951)

5. Match the actor to the movie in which he played a crooked cop.

_____	**1.** Sydney Greenstreet	**A.**	*Lady in the Lake*
_____	**2.** Robert Taylor	**B.**	*Private Hell 36*
_____	**3.** Glenn Ford	**C.**	*Touch of Evil*
_____	**4.** Lloyd Nolan	**D.**	*The Killing*
_____	**5.** Dana Andrews	**E.**	*I Wake up Screaming*
_____	**6.** Orson Welles		
_____	**7.** Laird Cregar	**F.**	*Sweet Smell of Success*
_____	**8.** Steve Cochran and Howard Duff	**G.**	*Where the Sidewalk Ends*
_____	**9.** Emile Meyer	**H.**	*Flamingo Road*
_____	**10.** Ted DeCorsia	**I.**	*The Money Trap*
		J.	*Rogue Cop*

QUIZ B

The following statements are either true or false. Score 3 points for each correct answer.

1. H.B. Warner played Inspector Nielsen of Scotland Yard in *Bulldog Drummond in Africa.* True or False?

2. Popeye Doyle, played by Gene Hackman in *The French Connection II*, becomes hooked on hard narcotics. True or False?

3. Two Los Angeles police detectives are killed when they turn over their weapons to two robbers in *The Onion Field.* True or False?

4. Sheriff Frank Hamer in *Bonnie and Clyde* was portrayed by Jack Elam. True or False?

5. Charles Cane, playing police Lieutenant Kincaid in *Dead Reckoning*, first meets Humphrey Bogart in an all-night diner. True or False?

6. William Bendix is Kirk Douglas' superior in *Detective Story*. True or False?

7. Captain Frank Nelson in *The Enforcer* (1951) was played by Roy Roberts. True or False?

8. Orson Welles played the Turkish Inspector Haki in *The Mask of Dimitrios*. True or False?

9. Kurt Katch played the Turkish Inspector Haki in *Journey Into Fear*. True or False?

10. The Scottish detective who refuses to believe Robert Donat's story in *The 39 Steps* is played by Frank Collier. True or False?

QUIZ C

Score 4 points for each correct answer.

1. In which of the following movies did Spencer Tracy play a law enforcement officer?

_____ **A.** *Disorderly Conduct*

_____ **B.** *Me and My Gal*

_____ **C.** *Whipsaw*

_____ **D.** All of the above.

2. Which actor played the dedicated but heartless cop opposite Humphrey Bogart in *The Great O'Malley?*

_____ **A.** Spencer Tracy

_____ **B.** Pat O'Brien

_____ **C.** James Cagney

3. The detective who builds the murder case against Humphrey Bogart in *In A Lonely Place* was played by

_____ **A.** Carl Benton Reid.

_____ **B.** Frank Lovejoy.

_____ **C.** Art Smith.

4. The detective investigating corruption in *On The Waterfront* was played by

_____ **A.** Dean Jagger.

_____ **B.** Leif Erickson.

_____ **C.** Walter Pidgeon.

5. As a detective, James Stewart contracts an abnormal fear while pursuing a robber in

_____ **A.** *Rear Window.*

_____ **B.** *The Man Who Knew Too Much.*

_____ **C.** *Vertigo.*

6. Chief Inspector Hubbard in *Dial M For Murder* was played by

_____ **A.** John Williams.

_____ **B.** Warren William.

_____ **C.** Rhys Williams.

7. Thomas J. Doyle, the detective in *Rear Window*, was played by

_____ **A.** MacDonald Carey.

_____ **B.** Wendell Corey.

_____ **C.** Jeff Corey.

8. Jack Grahame, the detective in *Shadow of A Doubt*, was played by

_____ **A.** MacDonald Carey.

_____ **B.** Wendell Corey.

_____ **C.** Jeff Corey.

9. James Cagney, in *Kiss Tomorrow Goodbye*, pays off Inspector Weber, who was played by

_____ **A.** Ward Bond.

_____ **B.** Barton MacLane.

_____ **C.** John Litel.

10. The detective who grills Humphrey Bogart in a diner in *Dark Passage* is played by

_____ **A.** Craig Kennedy.

_____ **B.** Arthur Kennedy.

_____ **C.** Douglas Kennedy.

QUIZ D

Match the movie cop to his profile. Score 5 points for each correct answer.

1. James McLeod

2. James "Brick" Davis

3. Harry Callahan

4. Buford Pusser

5. Popeye Doyle

_____ **A.** He is a Tennessee sheriff who takes on a local crime cartel despite vicious attacks on his family. His car explodes and his wife is mortally wounded from the bomb planted by thugs.

_____ **B.** A dedicated New York detective, he is undone when he learns that his wife has been impregnated by a mobster and has had an abortion performed by a quack he has arrested; he is killed by a psychopathic murderer.

_____ **C.** His legal education was paid for by a rackets kingpin and his best friend, played by Regis Toomey in the film, is killed by gangsters, which prompts him to join the F.B.I. and track down the killers.

_____ **D.** A rugged individualist, he is obsessed with tracking down narcotics pushers, which leads him to discover an international drug-smuggling ring.

_____ **E.** Three films have been based on this non-conforming San Francisco police detective, one who uses guns and fists to apprehend a host of arch-criminals.

QUIZ E

Name the motion pictures featuring policemen shown on the following pages. Score 5 points for each correct answer.

1. Surrounded by waitresses and hostess Gladys George,
Sydney Greenstreet, a thoroughly corrupt sheriff, is
shown in:

2. Clint Eastwood, as a tough cop, is in pursuit of drug pushers in:

3. Humphrey Bogart, with Mary Astor holding on for dear life, is ready for anything as an undercover army agent in:

4. Federal agent Cary Grant studies Ingrid Bergman in:

5. Charles Laughton, shown with Franchot Tone, is the relentless French Inspector Maigret in:

Scoring

Quiz A _____

Quiz B _____

Quiz C _____

Quiz D _____

Quiz E _____

Chapter Total Score _____

Your Police Detective Rating

If you scored between 370 and 333   You deserve to be appointed Police Commissioner.

If you scored between 332 and 277   Your name is on the parchment roll of honor at headquarters.

If you scored between 276 and 235   It's back to pounding a beat for you.

BAD WOMEN

They have been with us ever since Theda Bara vamped her way across the silent screen and Lya de Putti destroyed Emil Jannings in *Variety*. They are the femme fatales, the beautiful but vicious ladies who annihilate everyone and everything in their wicked paths. Moreover, in crime, perhaps there is nothing more alarming than to see a ravishing Gene Tierney reach out her milky arm to murder, or a sophisticated Barbara Stanwyck sink to the level of a back alley killing.

Hollywood's greatest actresses have aspired to play evil ladies, from bank robbers to murderesses, from whores (with hearts of gold, naturally) to harridans. Joan Crawford, Bette Davis, Susan Hayward, Rita Hayworth, Lana Turner have all turned in memorable performances as thieves, arsonists, blackmailers, extortionists, and killers.

Here, then, is a bevy of filmdom's high priestesses in a series of quizzes designed to jolt your memory and conjure shuddering images of lethal ladies at work.

QUIZ A

Score 5 points for each correct answer.

1. Match the actress and the movie with her criminal occupation.

_____ **1.** Joan Blondell in *Bullets or Ballots*	**A.** Spy
	B. Runs policy ring
_____ **2.** Bette Davis in *Marked Woman*	**C.** Prostitute
_____ **3.** Mary Astor in *The Maltese Falcon*	**D.** Killer
	E. Thief
_____ **4.** Signe Hasso in *The House on 92nd Street*	
_____ **5.** Lee Grant in *Detective Story*	

2. Match the actress to the film in which she portrayed bank robber and killer Bonnie Parker.

_____ **1.** Jean Harvey	**A.** *The Bonnie Parker Story*
_____ **2.** Patricia Morrison	
_____ **3.** Sylvia Sidney	**B.** *You Only Live Once*
_____ **4.** Peggy Cummins	**C.** *Persons In Hiding*
_____ **5.** Faye Dunaway	**D.** *Bonnie and Clyde*
_____ **6.** Dorothy Provine	**E.** *Gun Crazy*
	F. *Guns Don't Argue*

3. Match the actress to the film in which she played a role based on the infamous Ma Barker.

_____ **1.** Laurene Tuttle	**A.** *Queen of the Mob*

_____ **2.** Shelley Winters

_____ **3.** Blanche Yurka

_____ **4.** Margaret Wycherly

_____ **5.** Claire Trevor

B. *Ma Barker's Killer Brood*

C. *Bloody Mama*

D. *Untouchables*

E. *White Heat*

4. Match the actress to the film in which she served time in prison.

_____ **1.** Eleanor Parker

_____ **2.** Susan Hayward

_____ **3.** Lee Patrick

_____ **4.** Ellen Drew

_____ **5.** Bette Davis

A. *The Letter*

B. *Caged*

C. *Women Without Names*

D. *I Want To Live*

E. *Condemned Women*

5. Match the actress as criminal to the film based upon a Raymond Chandler story.

_____ **1.** Claire Trevor

_____ **2.** Jane Meadows

_____ **3.** Martha Vickers

_____ **4.** Charlotte Rampling

_____ **5.** Nancy Guild

A. *The Big Sleep (1946)*

B. *Farewell My Lovely*

C. *The Lady in the Lake*

D. *The Brasher Doubloon*

E. *Murder My Sweet*

QUIZ B

The following statements are either true or false. Score 3 points for each correct answer.

1. Gale Sondergaard portrayed the female villainess in Universal's Spider Woman series. True or False?

2. Bette Davis played the lethal Brigid O'Shaughnessy in the 1931 version of *The Maltese Falcon*. True or False?

3. Joan Crawford's role in *The Damned Don't Cry* was based on mob girl Virginia Hill. True or False?

4. Katrina Paxinou played a vicious harridan in *Confidential Agent* in which she forced a young girl to leap to her death from a high roof. True or False?

5. Agnes Moorehead was the sinister aide to Nazi Conrad Veidt in *All Through the Night*. True or False?

6. Agnes Moorehead was Humphrey Bogart's blackmailing girlfriend in *Dark Passage*. True or False?

7. Vera Miles is a thief in Hitchcock's *Psycho*. True or False?

8. Kim Novak played a dual murderess in Hitchcock's *Vertigo*. True or False?

9. Olivia de Havilland plans to murder Bette Davis in *My Cousin Rachel*. True or False?

10. Joan Crawford systematically murders her sister, Bette Davis, in *Whatever Happened to Baby Jane*? True or False?

QUIZ C

Score 4 points for each correct answer.

1. Elisha Cook's scheming wife in *The Killing* was played by

_____ **A.** Jean Hagen.

_____ **B.** Peggy Castle.

_____ **C.** Marie Windsor.

2. James Cagney's scheming wife in *White Heat* was played by

_____ **A.** Virginia Mayo.

_____ **B.** Virginia Bruce.

_____ **C.** Virginia Dare.

3. Paul Muni's scheming wife in *I Am A Fugitive From A Chain Gang* was played by

_____ **A.** Glenda Jackson.

_____ **B.** Glenda Farrell.

_____ **C.** Helen Vinson.

4. Ann Dvorak played the wayward sister of a gangster in

_____ **A.** *Bordertown.*

_____ **B.** *Black Fury.*

_____ **C.** *Scarface.*

5. Ann Dvorak played the jilted lover and gang girl in

_____ **A.** *G-Men.*

_____ **B.** *Come and Get It.*

_____ **C.** *Let 'Em Have It.*

_____ **D.** All of the above.

6. The vicious murderess in *The Paradine Case* was played by

_____ **A.** Ann Todd.

_____ **B.** Alida Valli.

_____ **C.** Ethel Barrymore.

7. The murderous thief whom Robert Mitchum falls in love with in *Out of the Past* is played by

_____ **A.** Rhonda Fleming.

_____ **B.** Jane Greer.

_____ **C.** Virginia Huston.

8. In which movie did Barbara Stanwyck send an innocent man to the gallows to cover up her killing of her aunt?

_____ **A.** *Cry Wolf*

_____ **B.** *The Other Love*

_____ **C.** *The Strange Loves of Martha Ivers*

9. Lizabeth Scott is proved to be a murderess in what film?

_____ **A.** *Dead Reckoning*

_____ **B.** *I Walk Alone*

_____ **C.** *You Came Along*

10. In *Strange Cargo* Joan Crawford plays a

_____ **A.** prostitute.

_____ **B.** thief.

_____ **C.** murderess.

QUIZ D

Match the profile to the actress and movie. Score 5 points for each correct answer.

1. Barbara Stanwyck in *Double Indemnity*

2. Bette Davis in *The Letter*

3. Joan Crawford in *This Woman is Dangerous*

4. Rita Hayworth in *Lady from Shanghai*

5. Gene Tierney in *Leave Her to Heaven*

_____ **A.** She shoots the man she loves because he is married to another. Then, to cover her crime, she claims her victim tried to rape her. She is finally stabbed to death by the victim's wife.

_____ **B.** The brains of a gang of robbers, she is the mistress of a maniacal killer, played by David Brian. Her eyesight fails and she falls in love with her doctor, which causes Brian to try to kill her. The F.B.I. kills Brian and the scarlet woman goes to jail, ostensibly to reform, return and marry her physician.

_____ **C.** She is a scheming, adulterous wife who conspires with a lover to murder her husband in order to collect his life insurance, then doublecrosses her lover, shooting him as he shoots her.

_____ **D.** Obsessed by her love for her husband, Cornel Wilde, she drowns his brother, kills her unborn child and then commits suicide.

_____ **E.** She is married to crippled Everett Sloane whom she drives crazy by cuckolding him and maddening him to the point where he tries to murder her.

QUIZ E

Name the motion picture from which stills are shown on the following pages depicting bad women. Score 5 points for each correct answer.

1. Faye Dunaway appears with Warren Beatty, about to rob another bank in:

2. Joan Fontaine (third from left) arrives with Laurence
Olivier at his country palace, Manderley, intimidated by
the host of servants greeting her, chiefly the vicious
housekeeper Judith Anderson in foreground. The film is:

3. Tough and lethal Leopoldine Konstantin advises her son, Claude Raines, to murder his wife, whom she suspects of being an agent, in:

4. Eleanor Parker is driven half-mad after becoming pregnant in prison. She is shown here in a scene from the movie:

5. A berserk Jessica Walter cutting Clint Eastwood to pieces in:

Scoring

Quiz A _____

Quiz B _____

Quiz C _____

Quiz D _____

Quiz E _____

Chapter Total Score _____

Your Femme Fatale Department Rating

If you scored between 250 and 225	No bad woman can get the better of you.
If you scored between 224 and 187	You're wary of wiley ladies but susceptible to their schemes.
If you scored between 186 and 125	Don't answer the phone, lock your door, and take up archeology.

GUNMEN & PEACEMAKERS

The violent heroes and heroines of the Old West still carry on America's tradition of the pioneer in films, an undying genre that was institutionalized in the first full-length motion picture, *The Great Train Robbery*, made by inventor Thomas Edison in 1903.

Since that time the Western has enthralled, thrilled, and generally delighted the American viewing audience, albeit the genre became more sophisticated as the decades passed, with psychological force working the motives and actions of the gunfighter and the sheriff who opposed him.

Here again, Hollywood draws heavily upon the real-life killers and lawmen of the Old West, profiling, sometimes with historical accuracy, the lives of Jesse James, Billy the Kid, the Daltons, the Youngers, Wyatt Earp, and company. The fictional sheriffs and gunfighters blasting their ways across the screen have appeared with equal authenticity, more so in the last three decades as the Western has been modernized for the eyes and ears of a less naive public.

The Western has given us larger-than-life heroes in the forms of Gary Cooper, John Wayne, Gregory Peck, Randolph Scott, and James Stewart to name only a few. And we have been awash with unforgettable western villains such as John Ireland, Arthur Kennedy, and Anthony Quinn. All of them have carved a niche on our memory, as the following quizzes should prove.

QUIZ A

Score 5 points for each correct answer.

1. Match the actor to the film in which he played Jesse James.

_____ **1.** Audie Murphy

_____ **2.** Tyrone Power

_____ **3.** MacDonald Carey

_____ **4.** Robert Wagner

_____ **5.** Robert Duval

A. *The True Story of Jesse James*

B. *The Great Missouri Raid*

C. *The Great Northfield, Minnesota, Raid*

D. *Jesse James*

E. *Kansas Raiders*

2. Match the actor to the film in which he played Billy the Kid.

_____ **1.** Robert Taylor

_____ **2.** Paul Newman

_____ **3.** Jack Buetel

_____ **4.** Johnny Mack Brown

A. *The Outlaw*

B. *Billy the Kid* (1941)

C. *The Left-Handed Gun*

D. *Billy the Kid* (1936)

3. Match the actor to the movie in which he played Wyatt Earp.

_____ **1.** Randolph Scott

_____ **2.** Joel McCrea

_____ **3.** Burt Lancaster

_____ **4.** Henry Fonda

_____ **5.** Walter Huston

A. *Gunfight at the O.K. Corral*

B. *Frontier Marshal*

C. *In Early Arizona*

D. *Law and Order*

E. *Wichita*

_____ **6.** Gordon Elliott   **F.** *My Darling Clementine*

4. Match the actor to the film in which he played a real-life outlaw.

_____ **1.** Steve McQueen

_____ **2.** Broderick Crawford

_____ **3.** Randolph Scott

_____ **4.** Dennis Morgan

_____ **5.** John Ericson

_____ **6.** Dan Duryea

A. *Al Jennings of Oklahoma*

B. *The Doolins of Oklahoma*

C. *Bad Men of Missouri* (Younger Brothers)

D. *The Return of Jack Slade*

E. *The Legend of Tom Horn*

F. *When the Daltons Rode*

5. Match the actor to the film in which he played a gunfighter.

_____ **1.** Alan Ladd

_____ **2.** Marlon Brando

_____ **3.** Gregory Peck

_____ **4.** Lee Marvin

_____ **5.** William S. Hart

A. *The Gunfighter*

B. *The Man Who Shot Liberty Valance*

C. *Hell's Hinges*

D. *Shane*

E. *The Missouri Breaks*

6. Match the actor to the movie in which he played a western bank robber.

_____ **1.** Gregory Peck

_____ **2.** John Wayne

_____ **3.** Marlon Brando

A. *Three Godfathers*

B. *One-Eyed Jacks*

C. *Yellow Sky*

_____ **4.** Stephen McNally   **D.** *Dark Command*

_____ **5.** Walter Pidgeon   **E.** *Winchester 73*

7. Match the actor to the movie in which he played a law man.

_____ **1.** John Wayne   **A.** *The Gunfighter*

_____ **2.** Millard Mitchell   **B.** *Rio Bravo*

_____ **3.** James Stewart   **C.** *The Tin Star*

_____ **4.** Henry Fonda   **D.** *Destry Rides Again*

_____ **5.** Gary Cooper   **E.** *Northwest Mounted Police*

QUIZ B

The following statements are either true or false. Score 3 points for each correct answer.

1. In *3:10 to Yuma* farmer Glenn Ford takes killer Van Heflin to prison via train. True or False?

2. In *Eldorado*, John Wayne has to sober up Robert Mitchum so he can properly assume his responsibilites as sheriff. True or False?

3. In a *Gunfight*, Kirk Douglas and Raf Vallone face each other in a much publicized show-down. True or False?

4. The cattle thief shot to death in *Mail Order Bride* (also entitled *West of Montana*) is played by Warren Oates. True or False?

5. The gunman Cherry Valance in *Red River* is played by John Ireland. True or False?

6. Noah Beery, Jr., plays the lead role in *I Shot Jesse James*. True or False?

7. Frank Faylen plays the murderous Ike Clanton in *Gunfight at the O.K. Corral.* True or False?

8. In *Warlock,* gunfighter Henry Fonda is hired to clean up a gang-controlled town. True or False?

9. Joel McCrea is forced to kill his best friend Zachary Scott in *South of St. Louis.* True or False?

10. Stacy Keach plays Cole Younger in *The Long Riders.* True or False?

QUIZ C

Score 4 points for each correct answer.

1. Errol Flynn becomes the sheriff of a hell town after a child is killed in a shoot-out in

_____ **A.** *Viriginia City.*

_____ **B.** *Dodge City.*

_____ **C.** *Carson City.*

2. Gary Cooper, playing Wild Bill Hickok in *The Plainsman,* is shot by Jack McCall, portrayed by

_____ **A.** Porter Hall.

_____ **B.** Thurston Hall.

_____ **C.** James Hall.

3. *The Virginian* is played by

_____ **A.** Gary Cooper.

_____ **B.** Joel McCrea.

_____ **C.** Dustin Farnum.

_____ **D.** All of the above.

4. "If you want to call me that, smile," is a line from

_____ **A.** *The Texan.*

_____ **B.** *The Virginian.*

_____ **C.** *The Kansan.*

5. Gary Cooper plays a sheriff in

_____ **A.** *The Last Outlaw.*

_____ **B.** *Dallas.*

_____ **C.** *Springfield Rifle.*

_____ **D.** All of the above.

6. The killers in *Desperate Siege* (originally entitled *Rawhide*) are played by

_____ **A.** George Tobias.

_____ **B.** Hugh Marlowe.

_____ **C.** Jack Elam.

_____ **D.** All of the above.

7. Whip McCord, the gunslinging killer who heads up a gang of killers in *The Oklahoma Kid*, is played by

_____ **A.** James Cagney.

_____ **B.** Humphrey Bogart.

_____ **C.** George Raft.

8. In *The Shootist,* aging gunfighter John Wayne is dying of

_____ **A.** bullet wounds.

_____ **B.** cancer.

_____ **C.** tuberculosis.

9. The robber-killer in *Hombre* is played by

_____ **A.** Richard Boone.

_____ **B.** Richard Widmark.

_____ **C.** Richard Todd.

10. James Stewart's traitorous gunslinger friend in *Bend in the River* is played by

_____ **A.** Jack Lambert.

_____ **B.** Arthur Kennedy.

_____ **C.** John McIntyre.

QUIZ D

Match the movie to the westerner's profile. Score 5 points for each correct answer.

1. *The Westerner*

2. *Angel and the Badman*

3. *Magnificent Seven*

4. *The Gunfighter.*

5. *The Fastest Gun Alive*

_____ **A.** Considered the top gun in the West, this gunslinger arrives in a peaceful town and is called out to face down another fast gun who challenges him. He kills the challenger but stays on to live anonymously in the community, the townsfolk burying his reputation in an empty grave.

_____ **B.** Considered the top gun in the West, this gunman arrives in a peaceful town to see his small son. He overstays his welcome and is shot down by the town's gun bully.

_____ **C.** This notorious gunman meets a Quaker girl and falls in love with her. Through her subtle ways the girl totally reforms the gunslinger.

_____ **D.** This notorious gunman meets a farm girl and sides with her people against the cattlemen and a crazy self-styled judge whom he eventually kills.

_____ **E.** He is a notorious gunman who organizes a group of gunslingers to defend a small Mexican town against a marauding band of ruthless bandits.

QUIZ E

Name the western movie depicted in the visual quiz on the follwoing pages. Score 5 points for each correct answer.

1. James Garner and Jason Robards are two of the fierce foursome who march to the O.K. Corral in:

2. With Grace Kelly prone in the street between them, Ian
MacDonald and Gary Cooper shoot it out in the classic:

3. Robert Redford gives a wounded Paul Newman cover-
ing fire in:

4. Manning a machine-gun is William Holden, with a mortally wounded Ernest Borgnine behind him in Sam Peckinpah's bloody film:

5. A one-eyed John Wayne draws a bead on two badmen
in:

Scoring

Quiz A _____

Quiz B _____

Quiz C _____

Quiz D _____

Quiz E _____

Chapter Total Score _____

Your Gunslinger Rating

If you scored between 300 and 270   You're a match for Billy the Kid.

If you scored between 269 and 225   You've earned a deputy sheriff's badge.

If you scored between 224 and 150   When they ask for volunteer possemen, don't raise your hand.

BEHIND THE
GRAY WALLS

The prison picture, though not currently enjoying the vogue it had during the 1930s and 1940s, has earned a place in Hollywood's hall of fame. To be sure, modern films about prison and prisoners still enjoy widespread interest, with audiences flocking to see *Brubaker*, *On the Yard* and *Escape From Alactraz*, to name only a few of the recent films dealing with an endlessly fascinating subject.

For most crime movie fans, the classic prison pictures are those in which Edward G. Robinson, George Raft, James Cagney and Humphrey Bogart strutted and swaggered in prison gray suits, furtively planning revenge on informers and prison breaks. It was behind the gray walls that Hollywood built where many of us in early youth **came to know the realistic punishments waiting for *us*** should we break the law of the land (or that decreed by Jack Warner). The movies, irrespective of their exploitation of a sensational subject, did bring about through their starkly realistic approach, significant prison reforms, and it is an accepted fact that Hollywood shamed the disgraceful chain gangs of the Old South out of existence through films made by Mervyn LeRoy and Preston Sturges.

The following quizzes should spark the reader's recall of those films where cons snarled in the yard, guards nervously fingered nightsticks, and sweaty wardens waited for the sirens to signal disaster.

QUIZ A

Score 5 points for each correct answer.

1. Match the prison movie to the actor who played the warden.

_____	**1.** Robert Redford	**A.**	_Unchained_
_____	**2.** Arthur Byron	**B.**	_Each Dawn I Die_
_____	**3.** Lewis Stone	**C.**	_Brute Force_
_____	**4.** George Bancroft	**D.**	_Riot in Cell Block Eleven_
_____	**5.** Walter Huston		
_____	**6.** Roman Bohnen	**E.**	_The Big House_
_____	**7.** Emile Meyer	**F.**	_The Criminal Code_
_____	**8.** Chester Morris	**G.**	_Brubaker_
_____	**9.** Patrick McGoohan	**H.**	_20,000 Years in Sing Sing_
_____	**10.** Martin Gabel		
_____	**11.** Humphrey Bogart	**I.**	_There Was A Crooked Man_
_____	**12.** James Cagney		
_____	**13.** Joseph King	**J.**	_Escape from Alcatraz_
_____	**14.** Karl Malden		
_____	**15.** Tom Tully	**K.**	_Mayor of Hell_
		L.	_Crime School_
		M.	_Birdman of Alcatraz_
		N.	_Behind the High Wall_
		O.	_San Quentin_

2. Match the method of escape used by convicts to the prison movie.

_____ **1.** _Big House, U.S.A._ **A.** Floated away on raft

_____ **2.** *White Heat*

_____ **3.** *Johnny Apollo*

_____ **4.** *Count of Monte Cristo*

_____ **5.** *Midnight Express*

_____ **6.** *The Great Escape*

_____ **7.** *On the Yard*

_____ **8.** *Strange Cargo*

_____ **9.** *Papillion*

_____ **10.** *Passage to Marseille*

_____ **11.** *Dark Passage*

_____ **12.** *I Am A Fugitive From A Chain Gang*

_____ **13.** *Blackmail*

_____ **14.** *San Quentin*

_____ **15.** *You Can't Get Away With Murder*

B. Through boiler system of prison

C. Substitutes self for dead prisoner

D. In balloon

E. Six escape through swamp to boat

F. Five escape in canoe

G. In prison garbage truck

H. In a dump truck

I. In a boxcar

J. From a road gang

K. Under a truck

L. Through elaborate tunnel

M. Dressed in guard's uniform

N. Through prison laundry

O. In doctor's car

3. Match the prison movie to the actor playing the convict.

_____ **1.** Burt Lancaster

_____ **2.** Spencer Tracy

_____ **3.** Humphrey Bogart

_____ **4.** James Cagney

_____ **5.** Neville Brand

A. *Inside the Walls of Folsom Prison*

B. *San Quentin*

C. *The Big House*

D. *Castle on the Hudson*

_____ **6.** Steve Cochran
_____ **7.** Wallace Beery
_____ **8.** Edward G. Robinson
_____ **9.** John Garfield
_____ **10.** George Raft

E. *House Across the Bay*

F. *20,000 Years in Sing Sing*

G. *The Last Gangster*

H. *Each Dawn I Die*

I. *Riot in Cell Block Eleven*

J. *Brute Force*

4. Match the actor to the prison movie in which he is executed.

_____ **1.** Clark Gable
_____ **2.** James Cagney
_____ **3.** Spencer Tracy
_____ **4.** John Garfield
_____ **5.** Susan Hayward
_____ **6.** Ronald Coleman
_____ **7.** Paul Muni
_____ **8.** Edward G. Robinson
_____ **9.** Kerr Dullea
_____ **10.** George E. Stone

A. *20,000 Years in Sing Sing*

B. *I Want To Live*

C. *Angels with Dirty Faces*

D. *A Tale of Two Cities*

E. *Two Seconds*

F. *The Last Mile*

G. *The Hoodlum Priest*

H. *Manhattan Melodrama*

I. *The Postman Always Rings Twice* (1946)

J. *The Valiant*

5. Match the sadistic guard to the prison movie.

_____ **1.** Hope Emerson   **A.** *San Quentin*

_____ **2.** Barton MacLane   **B.** *Brute Force*

_____ **3.** Hume Cronyn   **C.** *Mayor of Hell*

_____ **4.** Willard Robertson   **D.** *Caged*

_____ **5.** Dudley Digges   **E.** *Each Dawn I Die*

QUIZ B

The following questions are either true or false. Score 3 points for each correct answer.

1. *Convicts Four* is the story of a prisoner rehabilitated through painting. True or False?

2. *My Six Convicts* is an offbeat film emphasizing prison humor. True or False?

3. Killer Fred MacMurray is shown dying in the gas chamber in *Double Indemnity*. True or False?

4. Clark Gable plays "Killer Mears" in *The Last Mile*. True or False?

5. William Campbell plays the real-life Caryl Chessman in *Cell 2455, Death Row*. True or False?

6. In *Buried Loot* (1935), Robert Taylor escapes from prison dressed as a priest. True or False?

7. Glenn Ford, a hardened con, leads the mass break in *Men Without Souls*. True or False?

8. Jeff Corey, the informer in *Brute Force*, is punished for his treachery by being burned to death in the prison foundry. True or False?

9. Joe Downing, the informer "Limpy" in *Each Dawn I Die,* is knifed while the prisoners are watching a movie. True or False?

10. In *Brubaker*, the young, idealistic warden leaves the prison a much-hated man. True or False?

QUIZ C

Score 4 points for each correct answer.

1. Who tapes a gun under one of the witnesses' chairs which made possible Edward G. Robinson's escape from the electric chair in *Black Tuesday*?

_____ **A.** Warren Stevens

_____ **B.** Ivan Triesault

_____ **C.** Ray Teal.

2. Mickey Rooney strangles a guard to break out of death row in the remake of *The Last Mile* (1959). Who plays the guard?

_____ **A.** Ted DeCorsia

_____ **B.** Bob Steele

_____ **C.** Don Red Barry

3. To whom is Tony Curtis chained all through his escape from a southern prison in *The Defiant Ones*?

_____ **A.** Sidney Poitier

_____ **B.** Godfrey Cambridge

_____ **C.** James Earl Jones

4. In which prison film does Jack Palance play a dual role?

_____ **A.** *King of Alcatraz*

_____ **B.** *The House of Numbers*

_____ **C.** *Duffy of San Quentin*

5. Strother Martin, the captain of a southern prison farm in *Cool Hand Luke*, invariably excuses his brutality with the same tired line, which is

_____ **A.** "The trouble is that you cons don't listen."

_____ **B.** "What we got here is failure to communicate."

_____ **C.** "I'm only doing this for your own good."

6. Former stockbroker and convict Edward Arnold in *Johnny Apollo* has the prison job of

_____ **A.** librarian.

_____ **B.** riveter.

_____ **C.** gardener.

7. Prisoner Dustin Hoffman in *Papillion* hides his gems from other convicts in

_____ **A.** hollow dentures.

_____ **B.** his anal cavity.

_____ **C.** his socks.

8. Paul Muni in *I Am a Fugitive from a Chain Gang* escapes to see his girl, then slips into the night. "How do you live?" she calls after him. He answers from the darkness of the last scene:

_____ **A.** "On my savings."

_____ **B.** "With my mother."

_____ **C.** "I steal."

9. Newsman James Stewart in *Call Northside 777* tries to establish the innocence of a prison inmate played by

_____ **A.** Dane Clark.

_____ **B.** Richard Conte.

_____ **C.** John Garfield.

10. The mentally disturbed prisoner in *The High Wall* is played by

_____ **A.** Robert Taylor.

_____ **B.** Robert Young. .

_____ **C.** Robert Ryan.

QUIZ D

Match the movie to the prisoner's profile. Score 5 points for each correct answer.

1. *Carbine Williams*

2. *Cool Hand Luke*

3. *I Am a Fugitive from a Chain Gang*

4. *Brute Force*

5. *Escape from Alcatraz*

_____ **A.** A breezy lightweight prisoner in a southern chain gang, he refuses to conform to the harsh prison regulations, attempting to escape at every opportunity, for which he is punished severely, but he earns the respect of his peers.

_____ **B.** Arrested and imprisoned for moonshining, this convict spends all his spare time secretly putting together an invention that subsequently aids America's war effort (WW II).

_____ **C.** He is a gangleader who leads a desperate prison escape so he can join his ailing girlfriend. Joining him in the break is the boss of the cons, played by Charles Bickford. The attempt fails, with all the principals killed.

_____ **D.** A cunning convict who decides to escape after another prisoner loses his painting privileges and chops off his fingers, he and two others escape through a ventilating system.

_____ **E.** Sent to a chain gang for a crime he did not commit, he is beaten and degraded to the point where he escapes. He finds work but is turned in and sent back to the chain gang from which he again escapes to lead a life in the underworld.

QUIZ E

Name the prison movie depicted in the visual quiz on the following pages. Score 5 points for each correct answer.

1. Humphrey Bogart and fellow con Joseph Sawyer are pried loose in the prison yard of:

2. Priest Pat O'Brien begs James Cagney, on his way to the chair, to die a coward so slum kids won't think him a hero in:

3. James Cagney and George Raft are behind bars in:

4. Burt Lancaster, his prison cell filled with canaries, plays
Robert Stroud in:

5. Sam Levine, who works as a reporter for the prison newspaper is about to take a beating from Hume Cronyn in:

Scoring

Quiz A _____

Quiz B _____

Quiz C _____

Quiz D _____

Quiz E _____

Chapter Total Score _____

Your Captain of the Guard Rating

If you scored between 395 and 355   You can walk anywhere in the yard without a nightstick.

If you scored between 354 and 296   You had better take along a pistol or two.

If you scored between 295 and 197   Don't step out of the guards' tower for a second.

MURDER MOST FOUL AND OTHERWISE

Perhaps no other subject so evokes public fascination as homicide, either in subtle or blatant form. Hollywood's murderers, and those who tracked them to earth and justice, have ranged from the maniacal to the charming, as Ernest Borgnine and Joseph Cotton aptly prove.

Many of Hollywood's successful murder movies have been based upon the exploits of real killers, from Jack the Ripper to Landru, the infamous Bluebeard, but equally as many have been drawn from the fictional pages of Poe, Stevenson and Wilkie Collins. What has made them come alive, of course, were the unforgettable performances of Joan Crawford, Bette Davis, Sydney Greenstreet, Peter Lorre, and hosts of others. Who could ever forget the panicking Lorre in *The Beast with Five Fingers*, who is vexed to madness by the undying hand of the man he has slain? Or the always sinister and lurking presence of *The Phantom of the Opera*, or the released convict lying in homicidal wait to kill his former prosecutor, or berserk gangster killers such as Tommy Udo about whom Victor Mature remarks in *Kiss of Death* to D.A. Brian Donlevy, "He's crazy and he's still smarter than you are!"

QUIZ A

Score 5 points for each correct answer.

1. Match the movie to the actor who played Jack the Ripper.

_____ **1.** Jack Palance   **A.** *The Lodger* (1926)

_____ **2.** Laird Cregar   **B.** *The Man Upstairs*

_____ **3.** Ivor Novello   **C.** *The Lodger* (1944)

2. Match the role played by Sydney Greenstreet to the murder mystery in which he appeared.

_____ **1.** Jerome K. Arbutny   **A.** *The Maltese Falcon*

_____ **2.** Casper Gutman   **B.** *Three Strangers*

_____ **3.** Count Fosco   **C.** *The Mask of Dimitrios*

_____ **4.** Mr. Peters

                                                  D. *The Woman in White*

3. Match the husband to the film in which he plans to murder his wife.

_____ **1.** Charles Boyer   **A.** *The Shining*

_____ **2.** Humphrey Bogart   **B.** *Gaslight*

_____ **3.** Burt Lancaster   **C.** *Conflict*

_____ **4.** Jack Nicholson   **D.** *Night of the Hunter*

_____ **5.** Robert Mitchum   **E.** *Sorry, Wrong Number*

_____ **6.** Joseph Cotton   **F.** *Love From a Stranger*

_____ **7.** Basil Rathbone   **G.** *Niagara*

4. Match the wife to the film in which she plans to murder her husband.

_____ **1.** Lana Turner	**A.** _Double Indemnity_
_____ **2.** Barbara Stanwyck	**B.** _The Killers_
_____ **3.** Bette Davis	**C.** _Bloody Mama_
_____ **4.** Ava Gardner	**D.** _The Postman Always Rings Twice_ (1946)
_____ **3.** Shelley Winters	
	E. _The Little Foxes_

5. Match the psychopathic peculiarity to the killer.

_____ **1.** Peter Lorre in _M_	**A.** Murders criminals
_____ **2.** Richard Widmark in _Kiss of Death_	**B.** Carries victim's head around in a hatbox
_____ **3.** Robert Montgomery in _Night Must Fall_	**C.** Kills deformed people
_____ **4.** George Brent in _The Spiral Staircase_	**D.** Kills woman in wheelchair by pushing her down stairs
_____ **5.** Charles Bronson in _Death Wish_	**E.** Murders children

6. Match the movie to the woman-killer.

_____ **1.** Michael Caine	**A.** _No Way To Treat a Lady_
_____ **2.** Rod Steiger	**B.** _Frenzy_
_____ **3.** Tony Curtis	**C.** _Dressed to Kill_
_____ **4.** Barry Foster	**D.** _Shadow of a Doubt_
_____ **5.** Joseph Cotton	**E.** _While the City Sleeps_
_____ **6.** John Drew Barrymore	**F.** _The Boston Strangler_

7. Match the movie to the psychopathic gangster killer.

_____ **1.** Eli Wallach   **A.** _The Big Heat_

_____ **2.** Joseph Wiseman   **B.** _Murder Inc._

_____ **3.** Lee Marvin   **C.** _The Enforcer_ (1951)

_____ **4.** Jack Lambert   **D.** _The Line Up_

_____ **5.** Peter Falk   **E.** _Detective Story_

8. Match the actor to the movie which dealt with a sensational murder trial.

_____ **1.** James Stewart   **A.** _Knock on Any Door_

_____ **2.** Claude Rains   **B.** _Twelve Angry Men_

_____ **3.** Orson Welles   **C.** _Compulsion_

_____ **4.** Lee J. Cobb   **D.** _Crime Without Passion_

_____ **5.** Humphrey Bogart

                                  E. _Anatomy of a Murder_

9. Match the movie to the psychopathic killer.

_____ **1.** Wendell Corey   **A.** _In Cold Blood_

_____ **2.** Robert Blake   **B.** _Crossfire_

_____ **3.** Albert Dekker   **C.** _The Killer Is Loose_

_____ **4.** Robert Mitchum   **D.** _Among the Living_

_____ **5.** Robert Ryan   **E.** _Cape Fear_

10. Match the actor or actress to the murder films of director Fritz Lang.

_____ **1.** Edward G. Robinson **A.** _Secret Beyond the Door_

_____ **2.** Margaret Lindsay

_____ **3.** Michael Redgrave   **B.** _House by the River_

_____ **4.** Louis Hayward

_____ **5.** Anne Baxter

_____ **6.** Glenn Ford

_____ **7.** Joan Fontaine

C. *Beyond a Reasonable Doubt*

D. *Human Desire*

E. *Scarlet Street*

F. *Woman in the Window*

G. *The Blue Gardenia*

11. Match the actor or actress to the films of Agatha Christie's murder tales.

_____ **1.** Ann Harding

_____ **2.** Barry Fitzgerald

_____ **3.** Tyrone Power

_____ **4.** David Niven

_____ **5.** Ingrid Bergman

A. *Witness for the Prosecution*

B. *Love from a Stranger*

C. *And Then There Were None*

D. *Murder on the Orient Express*

E. *Death on the Nile*

12. Match the actor to the films based upon Daphne du Maurier's tales of murder.

_____ **1.** Richard Burton

_____ **2.** Alec Guinness

_____ **3.** Donald Sutherland

A. *My Cousin Rachel*

B. *Don't Look Now*

C. *The Scapegoat*

13. Match the actor or actress to the films based upon the murder stories of Edgar Allan Poe.

_____ **1.** Maria Montez

_____ **2.** Karl Malden

A. *Murders in the Rue Morgue* (1971)

_____ **3.** Jason Robards, Jr.   **B.** *The Mystery of Marie Roget*

                                             C. *Phantom of the Rue Morgue*

14. Match the actress to the Hitchcock murder film in which she appeared.

_____ **1.** Vera Miles   **A.** *The Wrong Man*

_____ **2.** Ingrid Bergman   **B.** *Spellbound*

_____ **3.** Marlene Dietrich   **C.** *Stage Fright*

15. Match the actor to the film of Gaston Leroux's murderous phantom.

_____ **1.** Lon Chaney   **A.** *Phantom of the Paradise*

_____ **2.** Claude Rains

_____ **3.** Herbert Lom   **B.** *Phantom of the Opera* (1926)

_____ **4.** William Finley

                                             C. *Phantom of the Opera* (1962)

                                             D. *Phantom of the Opera* (1943)

QUIZ B

The following statements are either true or false. Score 3 points for each correct answer.

1. Raymond Burr played a vicious killer in *Red Light* (1949) who dropped a semi-truck on top of Gene Lockhart. True or False?

2. David Wayne played the child-killer in the 1950 remake of *M*. True or False?

3. The charming Uncle Charlie, woman-killer in Hitchcock's *Shadow of a Doubt*, was played by John Wayne. True or False?

4. Ralph Bellamy was the nightmare-haunted killer in *Blind Alley*. True or False?

5. Night of the Hunter, the story of a psychopathic killer, was directed by Charles Laughton. True or False?

6. Humphrey Bogart murders one wife and tries to kill his second spouse in *The Two Mrs. Carrolls* by arranging car accidents. True or False?

7. Clifton Webb murders William Bendix in *The Dark Corner* by pushing him in front of a subway train. True or False?

8. Killer Edmund Gwen attempts to murder Joel McCrea in *Foreign Correspondent* by pushing him in front of a subway train. True or False?

9. The killer in Brian De Palma's *Dressed to Kill* is a transvestite. True or False?

10. Sylvester Stallone apprehends a psychopathic killer in *Nighthawks* by dressing as a woman. True or False?

11. Edmund O'Brien in *D.O.A.* attempts to track down his own murderer before fatal poison takes effect. True or False?

12. Charles Bickford tracks down the subtle killer in *Fallen Angel*. True or False?

13. Robert Walker, as Bruno in *Strangers on a Train*, is plagued by an oddball killer, played by Farley Granger, who insists they swap murders. True or False?

14. Alfred Hitchcock's *Rope* was based upon the Lindbergh kidnapping-murder case. True or False?

15. Hitchcock's *I Confess* dealt with a young priest played by Montgomery Clift who had committed murder. True or False?

16. Alan Ladd made his first major film appearance as Grahame Green's deformed killer Raven in *This Gun for Hire*. True or False?

17. In the comedic *Kind Hearts and Coronets* Alec Guinness does away with a bevy of relatives. True or False?

18. The killer in *The List of Adrian Messenger* who eliminates his relatives one by one to inherit the family fortune is played by Frank Sinatra. True or False?

19. Charles McGraw and Leo Gordon play the roles of the two murderers in a film version of Hemingway's *The Killers* (1946). True or False?

20. In *Cruising*, Al Pacino is an undercover cop looking for a killer who preys upon S&M homosexuals. True or False?

QUIZ C

Score 4 points for each correct answer.

1. The sadistic killer Jeff in the 1935 version of *The Glass Key* is portrayed by

_____ **A.** William Bendix.

_____ **B.** Guinn "Big Boy" Williams.

_____ **C.** Jack Pennock.

2. The conspiratorial murders in *Double Indemnity* are

_____ **A.** Myrna Loy and Clark Gable.

_____ **B.** Fred MacMurray and Barbara Stanwyck.

_____ **C.** Burt Lancaster and Yvonne de Carlo.

3. Jack Palance's first major role was in the murder film

_____ **A.** *Kiss of Fire.*

_____ **B.** *Sudden Fear.*

_____ **C.** *Flight to Tangier.*

4. The sophisticated killer in *Laura*, portrayed by Clifton Webb, is named

_____ **A.** Elwood P. Dowd.

_____ **B.** Joseph Tura.

_____ **C.** Waldo Lydecker.

5. *The Hatchet Man* (1932), a compassionless Chinese tong killer, was played by

_____ **A.** Warner Oland.

_____ **B.** Sidney Toler.

_____ **C.** Edward G. Robinson.

6. Character actor Donald Crisp portrayed which alcoholic killer in D. W. Griffith's masterpiece *Broken Blossoms* (1919)?

_____ **A.** Battling Levinsky

_____ **B.** Battling Burrows

_____ **C.** Battling Nelson

7. Luke Hatfield, the degenerate murderer in *Tol'able David* (1921) is portrayed by

_____ **A.** Walter Long.

_____ **B.** George Siegmann.

_____ **C.** Ernest Torrence.

8. The brutal killer "Deadlegs" Flint in *Kongo* (1932) is portrayed by

_____ **A.** Walter Huston.

_____ **B.** Lon Chaney.

_____ **C.** Ralph Ince.

9. The xenophobic killer in *Bad Day at Black Rock* is played by

_____ **A.** Robert Ryan.

_____ **B.** Ernest Borgnine.

_____ **C.** Lee Marvin.

10. Captain Lesgate, the would-be killer-for-hire of Grace Kelly in *Dial M for Murder*, is portrayed by

_____ **A.** Ray Milland.

_____ **B.** Anthony Dawson.

_____ **C.** Herbert Lom.

11. An invalided James Stewart thinks he has uncovered a murder in *Rear Window*. Who is his homicidal neighbor?

_____ **A.** Buddy Ebsen

_____ **B.** Raymond Burr

_____ **C.** Richard Boone

12. Rondo Hatton plays the same killer in several films. He is called

_____ **A.** The Creeper.

_____ **B.** The Crawler.

_____ **C.** The Climber.

13. The boy who witnesses a murder and whom no one will believe in *The Window* is played by

_____ **A.** Bobby Breen.

_____ **B.** Bob Watson.

_____ **C.** Bobby Driscoll.

14. The murderous vagrant in *The Hitchhiker* is played by

_____ **A.** Raymond Burr.

_____ **B.** William Talman.

_____ **C.** William Hopper.

15. Anthony Perkins in *Psycho* dresses up in

_____ **A.** his mother's clothes.

_____ **B.** his grandmother's clothes.

_____ **C.** his sister's clothes.

QUIZ D

Match the movie killer to his profile. Score 5 points for each correct answer.

1. Laird Cregar in *Hangover Square*

2. Joan Fontaine in *Ivy*

3. Frank Sinatra in *Suddenly*

4. Joan Crawford in *Berserk*

5. Humphrey Bogart in *In a Lonely Place*

_____ **A.** She marries a well-to-do man, but becomes alarmed when she discovers that his fortune is dwindling. This beautiful but thoroughly corrupt woman then meets another man of wealth and, to marry him, proceeds to murder her husband by poisoning him.

_____ **B.** He is a script writer in Hollywood, a man of violent temper who beats up producers and slaps his agent around. When a girl he invites home is later murdered he becomes the prime suspect, even in the mind of his sweetheart.

_____**C.** Based on a Patrick Hamilton novel, this is the story of London during the gaslight era and deals with a brilliant composer who suffers losses of memory; during one of these blackouts he murders a singer he loves and throws her bundled corpse onto a Guy Fawkes Day bonfire.

_____**D.** He is a ruthless, dedicated killer who lays in wait for an important government figure to kill him and no amount of cajoling and pleading from his captives will seemingly alter his plans of assassination.

_____**E.** She owns a traveling circus and has a maniacal daughter who begins killing members of the troupe out of insane jealousy for her mother who, she later states, neglected her as a child.

QUIZ E

Name the murder movie depicted in the following visual quiz. Score 5 points for each correct answer.

1. Alan Arkin chases the blind Audrey Hepburn in a tense scene from:

2. Barry Foster, a psychopathic killer, attacks Barbara Leigh-Hunt in Alfred Hitchcock's:

3. Martha Ray pitches woo to Charlie Chaplin as one of his many wives, murder victims all, in Chaplin's portrayal of French killer Landru, the infamous Bluebeard, in:

4. Humphrey Bogart, shown with Walter Huston, contemplates murder to protect the gold he has dug out of a mountain in:

5. A terrified Doris Day clings to husband Rex Harrison as they examine a mysterious tape recorder in their apartment after she has received innumerable death threats in:

Scoring

Quiz A   _____

Quiz B   _____

Quiz C   _____

Quiz D   _____

Quiz E   _____

    Chapter Total Score   _____

Your Homicide Squad Rating

If you scored between 520 and 468   Would-be killers will shrink at at the sight of your shadow.

If you scored between 467 and 390   It will take a few strong clues but you'll get your man.

If you scored between 389 and 260   You'd do as well to see a competent soothsayer.

INSIDE THE
OUTFIT

With the revelation in the late 1930s of the existence of a national crime cartel, chiefly through the uncovering of Lepke's Murder, Inc., Hollywood slowly began to produce movies dealing with the syndicate in one form or another. During the 1950s, the crime cartel was portrayed as a vague group of racketeers loosely organized under a single rackets chief, whether he be Luther Adler or, in the remake of *The Killers*, Ronald Reagan. As the presence of the Mafia (or Cosa Nostra as it was called in the East) came to full and gruesome light, Hollywood embarked upon a series of films that showed this lethal brotherhood in all its heinous forms.

Not until Mario Puzo's excellent *The Godfather* came to the screen, however, was the far-reaching omnipotency of the Mafia realized. Here an entire new breed of actors came to stardom—Al Pacino, Robert DeNiro and others—and since their appearance in this one Mafia epic, they have fairly dominated the screen.

The following quizzes deal with those sinister characters who populate the films dealing with the all-powerful and very real crime syndicate.

QUIZ A

Score 5 points for each correct answer.

1. Match the actor to the film in which he played a crime syndicate leader.

_____	**1.** Kirk Douglas	**A.** *Crazy Joe*
_____	**2.** Lee J. Cobb	**B.** *The Enforcer*
_____	**3.** Marlon Brando	**C.** *Lepke*
_____	**4.** Robert DeNiro	**D.** *New York Confidential*
_____	**5.** Luther Adler	
_____	**6.** John Payne	**E.** *Mickey One*
_____	**7.** Everett Sloan	**F.** *On the Waterfront*
_____	**8.** Tony Curtis	**G.** *The Brotherhood*
_____	**9.** Broderick Crawford	**H.** *The Godfather, Part I*
_____	**10.** Hurd Hatfield	**I.** *The Godfather, Part II*
		J. *The Boss*

2. Match the actor to the film in which he played a syndicate hit man.

_____	**1.** Fred Williamson	**A.** *Crazy Joe*
_____	**2.** Bob Steele	**B.** *Murder, Inc.*
_____	**3.** Franco Lantieri	**C.** *Black Caesar*
_____	**4.** Martin Scorcese	**D.** *Murder by Contract*
_____	**5.** Peter Falk	**E.** *Underworld, U.S.A.*
_____	**6.** Lenny Montana	**F.** *The Enforcer* (1951)
_____	**7.** Vince Edwards	**G.** *Point Blank*
_____	**8.** Gianni Russo	**H.** *Mean Streets*

_____ **9.** Lee Marvin   **I.** *Lepke*

_____ **10.** Cliff Robertson   **J.** *The Godfather, Part I*

3. Match the movie to the site where a syndicate killing is committed.

_____ **1.** *Crazy Joe*   **A.** A farmhouse

_____ **2.** *Godfather, Part I*   **B.** In a car

_____ **3.** *The Enforcer* (1951)   **C.** Cafe specializing in clams

_____ **4.** *Godfather, Part II*

_____ **5.** *Mean Streets*   **D.** An Italian restaurant

    E. On the courthouse steps

4. Match the real life syndicate leader to the film in which he is profiled.

_____ **1.** Frank Costello   **A.** *Murder, Inc.*

_____ **2.** Louis "Lepke" Buchalter   **B.** *The Valachi Papers*

    C. *The Damned Don't Cry*

_____ **3.** Vito Genovese

_____ **4.** Charles "Lucky" Luciano   **D.** *Hoodlum Empire*

    E. *Marked Woman*

_____ **5.** Benjamin "Bugsy" Siegal

5. Match the actor to the part he played in *Godfather, Part I.*

_____ **1.** Al Lettieri   **A.** Bruno Tattaglia

_____ **2.** Tony Giorgio   **B.** Solezzo

_____ **3.** Richard Castellano   **C.** Tessio

_____ **4.** Abe Vigoda   **D.** Barzini

_____ **5.** Richard Conte   **E.** Clemanza

QUIZ B

The following statements are either true or false. Score 3 points for each correct answer.

1. In *The Brothers Rico* Larry Gates plays the mob boss. True or False?

2. Henry Silva in *Johnny Cool* is a loyal, fanatical killer for the syndicate. True or False?

3. Rip Torn plays Peter Boyle's brother in *Crazy Joe*. True or False?

4. *Inside the Mafia* stars Arthur Kennedy. True or False?

5. In *Godfather, Part I*, Fredo Corleone is machine-gunned to death at a tollway stop. True or False?

6. *Willy Dynamite* deals with syndicate involvement in narcotics smuggling. True or False?

7. Roy Scheider and Gene Hackman man a wire tap in *The French Connection*. True or False?

8. Roy Roberts plays the syndicate chieftain in *Deadline, U.S.A.* True or False?

9. Sean Connery must seek syndicate sanctions to commit a robbery in *The Anderson Tapes*. True or False?

10. Connie Corleone in *Godfather*, Parts I and II, is played by Diane Keaton. True or False?

QUIZ C

Score 4 points for each correct answer.

1. John Garfield's response to the syndicate chieftain after not having thrown the prizefight in *Body and Soul* is

_____ **A.** "Tell it to the Marines!"

_____ **B.** "Nobody lives forever!"

_____ **C.** "What are you gonna do—kill me? Everybody dies."

2. The syndicate goons backing up the crime boss in *On the Waterfront* are played by

_____ **A.** Tami Mauriello.

_____ **B.** Tony Galento.

_____ **C.** Harry Guardino.

_____ **D.** All of the above.

3. The real life fighter portrayed in *The Harder They Fall* who is controlled by the syndicate is

_____ **A.** James J. Braddock.

_____ **B.** Primo Carnera.

_____ **C.** Stanley Ketchel.

4. The real life fighter portrayed in *Raging Bull* who takes a dive for the Mafia is

_____ **A.** Rocky Graziano.

_____ **B.** Jake Lamotta.

_____ **C.** Rocky Marciano.

5. The singer in *Godfather, Part I,* is played by

_____ **A.** Tony Bennett.

_____ **B.** Tony Martin.

_____ **C.** Al Martino.

6. John McIntyre tries to clean up a syndicate-controlled town in

_____ **A.** *Kansas City Confidential.*

_____ **B.** *The Phoenix City Story.*

_____ **C.** *The Houston Story.*

7. The actor who recants his testimony in *Godfather, Part II*, is played by

_____ **A.** Michael V. Gazzo.

_____ **B.** John Cazale.

_____ **C.** Tom Rosqui.

8. The ritual Mafia kiss is received by Alex Cord in

_____ **A.** *The Outfit.*

_____ **B.** *Hit!*

_____ **C.** *The Brotherhood.*

9. The crime cartel in *The Valachi Papers* is called

_____ **A.** The Mafia.

_____ **B.** The Camorra.

_____ **C.** The Cosa Nostra.

10. The syndicate chieftain in *The Racket* is played by

_____ **A.** Robert Mitchum.

_____ **B.** Robert Ryan.

_____ **C.** Robert Young.

QUIZ D

Match the film to the syndicate mobster portrayed. Score 5 points for each correct answer.

1. *The Gangster*
2. *The Big Heat*
3. *On the Waterfront*
4. *Slaughter on Tenth Avenue*
5. *The Valachi Papers*

_____ **A.** He is a lowly mobster in New York City who rises to some prominence through connections with an underworld brotherhood and later is marked for murder when he informs on the cartel's leaders.

_____ **B.** He is a New York hoodlum who begins to lose his nerve and thus his control over his gang until, finally, his men go over to another faction of the syndicate and he is murdered.

_____ **C.** A trial reveals that syndicate killers are behind the murder of a labor leader, which results in a terrific battle between longshoremen and mobsters.

_____ **D.** He is a labor leader who began as a dock worker, and, through the aid of the syndicate, he becomes a total dictator of his union, until one worker becomes an informer and subsequently beats him up.

_____ **E.** He is a cop investigating the suicide of a partner and uncovers several murders and the syndicate's near-total control of the police department.

QUIZ E

Pick the syndicate film in the visual quiz on the following pages. Score 5 points for each correct answer.

1. Kirk Douglas is a Mafia don marked for murder in:

2. Ernest Borgnine plays the real-life police detective Lt. Petrosino investigating the early-day Mafia in:

3. Al Pacino, Marlon Brando, James Caan, and John
Cazale make up the leading Mafia members in:

4. John Garfield, Beatrice Pearson, and Thomas Gomez are rogue members of the syndicate's numbers racket and bookmaking operations in:

5. Gene Kelly and Teresa Celli are victims who fight back
against organized Italian extortionists in:

Scoring

Quiz A _____

Quiz B _____

Quiz C _____

Quiz D _____

Quiz E _____

Chapter Total Score _____

Your Syndicated Historian Rating

If you scored between 295 and 265 You are a top-flight chronicler of the Outfit.

If you scored between 264 and 221 You can pick out the Mafioso from the flunkies of the mob.

If you scored between 220 and 147 You have trouble knowing the difference between the syndicate and the Elks.

THE CAPER

Thieves, talented or awkward, have long held a fascination for Hollywood which almost from the beginning of motion pictures began by chronicling the capers of Raffles and his minions. Almost all of moviedom's top stars have played roles of robbers pulling capers, or of the arch-villains who masterminded the robberies, from John Barrymore to Robert Redford.

Oddly enough, the jewel thief has proved to be most popular in the caper genre, most probably because he is a non-violent type of thief who lives and conducts his stealthy robberies through cunning and wit, displaying a wry sense of humor. The more brutal malefactors, however, have not been ignored, with ruthless bank robbers sharply displayed in movies such as *Violent Saturday*.

The following quizzes will undoubtedly spark the reader's memory in recalling those yeggmen and cat burglars who thrilled several generations of movie-goers.

QUIZ A

Score 5 points for each correct answer.

1. Match the caper to the movie.

_____ **1.** *Mr. 880*   **A.** Jewel heist

_____ **2.** *Dog Day Afternoon*   **B.** Kidnapping

_____ **3.** *Kiss of Death*   **C.** Train robbery

_____ **4.** *White Heat*   **D.** Bank robbery

_____ **5.** *Dead End*   **E.** Counterfeiting

2. Match the director to the film he directed which portrayed a caper.

_____ **1.** Stanley Kubrik   **A.** *The Asphalt Jungle*

_____ **2.** John Huston   **B.** *Rififi*

_____ **3.** Jules Dassin   **C.** *Ocean's Eleven*

_____ **4.** Richard Fleischer   **D.** *The Killing*

_____ **5.** Lewis Milestone   **E.** *Violent Saturday*

3. Match the actor to the movie in which he played a thief.

_____ **1.** James Caan   **A.** *Criss Cross*

_____ **2.** Tony Curtis   **B.** *Assault on the Queen*

_____ **3.** Brian Keith

_____ **4.** Cary Grant   **C.** *Armored Car Robbery*

_____ **5.** James Cagney   **D.** *Robbery*

_____ **6.** Burt Lancaster   **E.** *Grand Slam*

_____ **7.** Stanley Baker   **F.** *To Catch a Thief*

_____ **8.** Frank Sinatra

_____ **9.** Charles McGraw

G. *Thief*

_____ **10.** Edward G.
Robinson

H. *Five Against the
House*

I. *Kiss Tomorrow
Goodbye*

J. *Six Bridges to Cross*

4. Match the actor to the movie in which he played "Mr.
Big" (the planner of the caper).

_____ **1.** Sean Connery

A. *White Heat*

_____ **2.** Fred Clark

B. *North by Northwest*

_____ **3.** James Mason

C. *The Great Train
Robbery*

_____ **4.** Rudolph Klein-Rogge

D. *The Killing*

_____ **5.** Sterling Hayden

E. *The Testament of
Dr. Mabuse*

5. Match the actor to the film in which he played a jewel
thief.

_____ **1.** Robert Redford

A. *Raffles* (1931)

_____ **2.** Herbert Marshal

B. *Raffles* (1917)

_____ **3.** Melvyn Douglas

C. *Arsene Lupin
Returns*

_____ **4.** John Barrymore

D. *Hot Rock*

_____ **5.** Ronald Coleman

E. *Trouble in Paradise*

QUIZ B

The following questions are either true or false. Score 3
points for each correct answer.

1. Ernest Borgnine and Charleton Heston plan a huge gold robbery in *The Badlanders*. True or False?

2. Ali McGraw plays an undercover agent trying to pinpoint Steve McQueen's next robbery in *The Thomas Crown Affair*. True or False?

3. The thieves in *Rififi* are all caught after they turn on each other. True or False?

4. The wife of a murdered armored car guard spies for the police in *Payroll* to apprehend the thieves. True or False?

5. The thieves in *The Day They Robbed The Bank of England* are all ex-British soldiers. True or False?

6. In *Goldfinger* the object of the theft is a priceless painting in the Louvre. True or False?

7. In *The Split*, thieves plan to rob the L.A. Colliseum of gate receipts. True or False?

8. In *Topkapi*, ingenious thieves plan to abscond with a crown of jewels in an Istanbul museum. True or False?

9. *How To Steal a Million* was directed by Billy Wilder. True or False?

10. In *The Big Boodle*, Errol Flynn is kept busy tracking down counterfeiters. True or False?

QUIZ C

Score 4 points for each correct answer.

1. What does Al Pacino shout to spectators in *Dog Day Afternoon*?

_____ **A.** "Sing Sing! Sing Sing!"

_____ **B.** "Attica! Attica!"

_____ **C.** "Get those cops off my back!"

2. Included in the mob that sets out to rob the Monte Carlo gambling vaults in *Seven Thieves* are

_____ **A.** Edward G. Robinson.

_____ **B.** Eli Wallach.

_____ **C.** Rod Steiger.

_____ **D.** All of the above.

3. In *A Prize of Gold*, thieves plan to

_____ **A.** steal the gold in Berlin's largest bank.

_____ **B.** steal Hitler's hidden gold from the U.S. Military.

_____ **C.** steal an enormous gold bullion shipment from the Berlin Air-Lift.

4. The notorious *Raffles* is played by

_____ **A.** Cary Grant.

_____ **B.** David Niven.

_____ **C.** Douglas Fairbanks, Jr.

_____ **D.** All of the above.

5. Members of the *Lavender Hill Mob* include

_____ **A.** Alec Guinness.

_____ **B.** Stanley Holloway.

_____ **C.** Alastair Sim.

_____ **D.** All of the above.

6. Members of the bumbling gang of thieves in *The Lady Killers* include

_____ **A.** Alec Guinness.

_____ **B.** Peter Sellers.

_____ **C.** Herbert Lom.

_____ **D.** All of the above.

7. *A Nice Little Bank That Should be Robbed* starred

_____ **A.** Mickey Rooney.

_____ **B.** Warren Oates.

_____ **C.** Tom Ewell.

8. Richard Conte starred in a vicious trucking movie called

_____ **A.** *Robber's Roost.*

_____ **B.** *Thieve's Highway.*

_____ **C.** *They Drive by Night.*

9. In *Six Bridges to Cross*, the aim of the thieves is to

_____ **A.** rob a federal reserve bank.

_____ **B.** rob Tiffany's.

_____ **C.** rob Brink's.

10. The villains in *Raiders of the Lost Ark* are

_____ **A.** Nazis.

_____ **B.** Communists.

_____ **C.** PLO Terrorists.

QUIZ D

Match the profile of the thief to the movie in which he appears. Score 5 points for each correct answer.

1. *The Killing*
2. *Thief*
3. *The Thief*
4. *To Catch a Thief*
5. *The Steel Trap*

_____ **A.** He is an executive in a bank who can no longer resist the temptation of looting the vault. which he does. fleeing the country over a weekend. He changes his mind and returns to the bank on Monday morning. racing against time to return the money before he is discovered.

_____ **B.** For the receipts of a race-track. he plans an elaborate robbery which requires a psychopathic killer to shoot one of the horses during a race.

_____ **C.** He steals state secrets for the Communists but his feelings of guilt overcome him and he turns himself in; not one word of dialogue is spoken in this film.

_____ **D.** He is a top-notch jewel thief whose success causes him to join a syndicate backer who, in turn, betrays him and goads him into mass murder.

_____ **E.** He is a retired cat burglar living on the Riviera who is wrongly accused of committing a series of jewel thefts and who is driven to apprehend the real thief.

QUIZ E

Name the film depicting the caper in the following visual quiz. Score 5 points for each correct answer.

1. Humphrey Bogart, Lauren Bacall, Thomas Gomez, Edward G. Robinson, Claire Trevor, Lionel Barrymore and Dan Seymour await a gangster named Ziggy in:

2. Ali McGraw takes aim, with Steve McQueen advising, in:

3. Sam Jaffe, Sterling Hayden, Richard Whitmore (standing), and Anthony Caruso go over the plans of their caper in:

4. Frank Sinatra and Angie Dickinson in a scene from a
Las Vegas robbery film entitled:

5. Peter Falk and accomplice pause during a rooftop
reconnaissance of the building they intend to rob in:

Scoring

Quiz A   _____

Quiz B   _____

Quiz C   _____

Quiz D   _____

Quiz E   _____

   Chapter Total Score   _____

Your Caper Division Score

If you scored between 270 and 243   You'd be in and out of the vault in record time.

If you scored between 242 and 202   It would take weeks before police got on to your trail.

If you scored between 201 and 135   You'd be arrested just for looking at the jewels in the window.

MISCELLANEOUS MISCREANTS

The movies have made much of detectives, killers, gangsters, outlaws and syndicate henchmen, but they have not ignored other areas of crime that are important in the social fabric of American life, important in that rogues and rascals of these genres are constantly at their nefarious work, from the repugnant rapist to the amusing con man. Not to be ignored are the kidnappers, arsonists, and fanatics representing criminal secret societies who have plagued their fellow citizens about the world.

Classic performances of these miscreants have been rendered by such glowering and terrifying personalities as Eduardo Cianelli, Lee Marvin, Ray Milland, Steve Cochran, and Walter Slezak. The women, particularly Hollywood's top leading ladies, were not to be denied evil roles, chiefly as prostitutes or madams of brothels, from Sophia Loren to Joanne Woodward.

Assassins, spies, drug addicts, even the Devil himself, came to be portrayed in Hollywood's crime movies, presenting audiences with riveting performances that fire the memory to this day. The following quizzes deal with a wide assortment of villains and vixens and should provide the reader with challenging tests of intuition, memory and just plain nostalgia for some unforgettably bad people.

146

QUIZ A

Score 5 points for each correct answer.

1. Match the actress to the film in which she played a rape victim.

_____	**1.** Jane Wyman	**A.**	_Outrage_
_____	**2.** Vivien Leigh	**B.**	_Anatomy of a Murder_
_____	**3.** Lee Remick		
_____	**4.** Claire Bloom	**C.**	_Peyton Place_
_____	**5.** Diane Varsi	**D.**	_Town Without Pity_
_____	**6.** Christine Kaufmann	**E.**	_The Mark_
_____	**7.** Diane Cilento	**F.**	_Johnny Belinda_
_____	**8.** Sophia Loren	**G.**	_Two Women_
_____	**9.** Morgan Fairchild	**H.**	_A Streetcar Named Desire_
_____	**10.** Maria Schell	**I.**	_Waterhole #3_
		J.	_The Seduction_

2. Match the actor to the film in which he played a con man.

_____	**1.** George C. Scott	**A.**	_Lady Killer_
_____	**2.** Paul Newman	**B.**	_The Flim-Flam Man_
_____	**3.** James Cagney	**C.**	_The Honey Pot_
_____	**4.** Rex Harrison	**D.**	_The Lady Eve_
_____	**5.** Douglas Fairbanks, Jr.	**E.**	_Bedtime Story_
_____	**6.** Robert Redford	**F.**	_Only When I Larf_
_____	**7.** Laird Cregar	**G.**	_The Sting_
_____	**8.** Charles Coburn	**H.**	_Rings on Her Fingers_

_____ **9.** Marlon Brando

_____ **10.** Richard Attenborough

I. *The Hustler*

J. *The Young in Heart*

3. Match the actress to the film in which she played a prostitute or madam.

_____ **1.** Sophia Loren

_____ **2.** Nancy Kwan

_____ **3.** Melina Mercouri

_____ **4.** Shelley Winters

_____ **5.** Carroll Baker

_____ **6.** Elizabeth Taylor

_____ **7.** Joan Blondell

_____ **8.** Diane Cilento

_____ **9.** Rita Hayworth

_____ **10.** Marlene Dietrich

_____ **11.** Bette Davis

_____ **12.** Vivien Leigh

_____ **13.** Joan Bennett

_____ **14.** Shirley MacLaine

_____ **15.** Shirley Jones

_____ **16.** Inger Stevens

_____ **17.** Carol White

_____ **18.** Claire Trevor

_____ **19.** Joanne Woodward

_____ **20.** Jane Russell

A. *Rattle of a Simple Man*

B. *Shanghai Express*

C. *Dead End*

D. *Sylvia*

E. *The World of Suzy Wong*

F. *The Balcony*

G. *Butterfield 8*

H. *Waterloo Bridge*

I. *Manhunt*

J. *Five Card Stud*

K. *Poor Cow*

L. *The Revolt of Mamie Stover*

M. *The Lady L*

N. *Gaily, Gaily*

O. *Waterhole #3*

P. *Elmer Gantry*

Q. *Irma La Douce*

R. *Miss Sadie Thompson*

S. *Of Human Bondage*

T. *Three Faces of Eve*

4. Match the spy-master to the actor who portrayed him.

_____ **1.** Paul Lukas

_____ **2.** Herbert Marshall

_____ **3.** Godfrey Tearle

_____ **4.** Otto Krueger

_____ **5.** Claude Rains

A. Alexander Sebastian in _Notorious_

B. Dr. Hartz in _The Lady Vanishes_

C. Stephen Fisher in _Foreign Correspondent_

D. Professor Jordan in _The 39 Steps_

E. Charles Tobin in _Saboteur_

5. Match the actor to the film in which he played an assassin.

_____ **1.** Sheppard Strudwick

_____ **2.** John Derek

_____ **3.** Horst Buchholz

_____ **4.** John Barrymore

_____ **5.** John Lodge

A. _The Scarlet Empress_

B. _Rasputin and the Empress_

C. _Prince of Players_

D. _All the King's Men_

E. _Nine Hours to Rama_

QUIZ B

The following statements are either true or false. Score 3 points for each correct answer.

1. Sidney Poitier attacks and rapes an attractive teacher in _The Blackboard Jungle._ True or False?

2. James Coburn plays a cop tracking down con artists in *Dead Heat on a Merry-Go-Round.* True or False?

3. *A Bullet for Joey* deals with a kidnapping. True or False?

4. *City of Fear* deals with the smuggling of narcotics. True or False?

5. *The Abductors* is the story of an attempt to rob Lincoln's grave. True or False?

6. The newspaperman trying to expose a baby racket in *Abandoned* is played by Franchot Tone. True or False?

7. Robert Mitchum plays Katherine Hepburn's killer husband in *Undercurrent.* True or False?

8. The KKK killer in *Storm Warning* is played by Stephen McNally. True or False?

9. The killer in *Black Legion* is played by Dick Foran. True or False?

10. The part of the mad guru who urges his Thugs to "kill for the love of Kali" in *Gunga Din* is played by Abner Biberman. True or False?

QUIZ C

Score 4 points for each correct answer.

1. The clairvoyant who envisions murder in *Dead of Night* is played by

_____ **A.** Michael Redgrave.

_____ **B.** Richard Attenborough.

_____ **C.** John Mills.

2. The con man/promoter of London's underworld in *Night and the City* is played by

_____ **A.** Richard Basehart.

_____ **B.** Richard Widmark.

_____ **C.** Richard Crenna.

3. Dick Powell in *Johnny O'Clock* plays a

_____ **A.** gambler.

_____ **B.** narcotics peddler.

_____ **C.** blackmailer.

4. The actor who plays the informer in *The Friends of Eddie Coyle* is

_____ **A.** Robert Taylor.

_____ **B.** Robert Ryan.

_____ **C.** Robert Mitchum.

5. Gangster Robert Montgomery in *Ride the Pink Horse* seeks revenge through

_____ **A.** extortion.

_____ **B.** blackmail.

_____ **C.** arson.

6. Which actor plays narcotics smuggler Harry Lime in *The Third Man*?

_____ **A.** Gregory Peck

_____ **B.** Joseph Cotton

_____ **C.** Orson Welles

7. The Nazi spy in *Captain Carey, U.S.A.* is played by

_____ **A.** Francis Lederer.

_____ **B.** Helmut Dantine.

_____ **C.** Kurt Kreuger.

8. The Nazi spy in *Lifeboat* is played by

_____ **A.** Walter Slezak.

_____ **B.** William Bendix.

_____ **C.** Hume Cronyn.

9. The Nazi spy in *The White Tower* is played by

_____ **A.** Lloyd Nolan.

_____ **B.** Norman Lloyd.

_____ **C.** Lloyd Bridges.

10. The Russian spy in *The Conspirator* is played by

_____ **A.** Robert Taylor.

_____ **B.** Robert Ryan.

_____ **C.** Robert Young.

QUIZ D

Match the profile to the crime film. Score 5 points for each correct answer.

1. *Alias Nick Beal*

2. *The Man with the Golden Arm*

3. *The Crime of Dr. Crespi*

4. *Suspicion*

5. *Sunset Boulevard*

_____ **A.** He is a doctor who injects a paralyzing drug into the man who has stolen his sweetheart, then buries him alive. The film is based upon Edgar Allan Poe's "The Premature Burial."

_____ **B.** Ray Milland, a sinister, shadowy figure, attempts to corrupt Thomas Mitchell, urging him to murder an enemy; he is, apparently, the Devil himself.

_____ **C.** This is the story of a drug addict who attempts to kick the habit by withdrawing cold turkey, based on a Nelson Algren novel; Otto Preminger directed.

_____ **D.** An ambitious young scriptwriter becomes a gigolo to a washed-up silent screen star who kills him when he threatens to leave her.

_____ **E.** The story of a young, impressionable bride who comes to believe that her charming but scheming husband is planning to kill her.

QUIZ E

Name the film in the following visual quiz. Score 5 points for each correct answer.

1. Frank McHugh pours some bathtub gin for James Cagney, in a film about bootleggers entitled:

2. Dewey Martin and Humphrey Bogart are escaped
prisoners who menace a suburban family in:

3. Humphrey Bogart is wanted for murder but is aided in his quest for the real killer by Lauren Bacall in:

4. Tyrone Power, a one-time carnival barker and con man who claims to read minds, confronts psychologist Helen Walker in:

5. Clairvoyant Edward G. Robinson is about to predict
a murder in:

QUIZ F

Your final crime movie quiz requires special expertise. Name the films the criminals were *watching* in the following films. Score 10 points for each correct answer.

1. The robber-killer escapes into a drive-in in *White Heat* to see:

2. The outlaws in *Bonnie and Clyde* go to a theater after a robbery to see:

3. While a convict informer is knifed to death in the dark, the prisoners in *Each Dawn I Die* watch a movie called:

4. Chain gang members in *Sullivan's Travels* are watching a film shown in a small backwoods church and laughing at:

Scoring

Quiz A _____

Quiz B _____

Quiz C _____

Quiz D _____

Quiz E _____

Quiz F _____

Chapter Total Score _____

Your Miscreant File Rating

If you scored between 410 and 369   There is no type of crime that can baffle you.

If you scored between 368 and 307   You are an excellent back-up to the chief.

If you scored between 306 and 205   You should be helping the desk sergeant type up reports.

SOLUTIONS

SOLUTIONS

THE P.I.s

Quiz A

1.	1. B	2. C	3. E	4. A	5. D
2.	1. D	2. A	3. B	4. E	5. C
3.	1. B	2. G	3. C	4. E	5. A
	6. D	7. F			
4.	1. I	2. J	3. A	4. F	5. B
	6. D	7. C	8. G	9. E	10. H
5.	1. E	2. D	3. J	4. G	5. A
	6. B	7. I	8. C	9. H	10. F
6.	1. C	2. D	3. A	4. B	
7.	1. E	2. A	3. B	4. C	5. D
8.	1. C	2. A	3. B	4. E	5. D
9.	1. B	2. A	3. D	4. E	5. C
10.	1. C	2. D	3. A	4. E	5. B

Quiz B

1. True.   **2.** False. Donald Cook played the role in this first of the Ellery Queen movies; Bellamy played the detective in later productions.   **3.** Warren William played the role, appearing in three other Warner Bros. productions on Perry in 1935-36; Woods appeared only once as Mason, in the 1937 production of *The Case of the Stuttering Bishop.*   **4.** True.   **5.** False. The Falcon series originally starred George Sanders who tired of the role and turned it over to his real-life brother Tom

Conway, making the transition in the 1942 RKO film, *The Falcon's Brother.*   **6.** True.   **7.** True.   **8.** False. Only Granville played the role.   **9.** True. **10.** True.

Quiz C

1. B   **2.** D   **3.** B   **4.** C   **5.** B
6. D   **7.** C   **8.** C   **9.** A,C   **10.** A

Quiz D

1. E   **2.** B   **3.** D   **4.** A   **5.** C

Quiz E

1. *The Maltese Falcon*
2. *Look Out, Mr. Moto*
3. *The Gracie Allen Murder Case*
4. *Charlie Chan at Treasure Island*
5. *The Long Goodbye*

GANGSTERS & GUN MOLLS

Quiz A

1. 1. G   2. F   3. A   4. B   5. H
      6. I   7. E   8. J   9. C   10. D
2. 1. F   2. E   3. G   4. J   5. A
      6. I   7. B   8. H   9. C   10. D
3. 1. H   2. J   3. I   4. B   5. C
      6. D   7. E   8. G   9. A   10. F

4.	1. J	2. E	3. I	4. F	5. H
	6. D	7. B	8. G	9. A	10. C
5.	1. C	2. E	3. B	4. A	5. D
6.	1. C	2. A	3. B	4. E	5. D
7.	1. C	2. A	3. D	4. E	5. B
8.	1. D	2. A	3. B	4. C	5. E
9.	1. E	2. D	3. A	4. C	5. B
10.	1. B	2. E	3. C	4. A	5. D

Quiz B

1. False. Eduardo Cianelli played the role.   **2.** True.
3. True.   **4.** True.   **5.** False. Just the opposite;
Montgomery plays a gangster who inherits a British title.
6. False. The speech was James Cagney's in *White Heat*
about Steve Cochran.   **7.** True.   **8.** False. It was
an Edward G. Robinson gangster vehicle.   **9.** True.
10. True.

Quiz C

1. A   **2.** B   **3.** C   **4.** B   **5.** A
6. C   **7.** C   **8.** A   **9.** C*   **10.** C

*Though it appears in some scenes that the actor is flippping
a larger coin. Raft insisted in all authorized biographies
(*see George Raft* by Lewis Yablonsky, pp. 67-68) that it
was a nickel.

Quiz D

1. C.   **2.** D   **3.** E   **4.** A   **5.** B

Quiz E

1. *Underworld*

2. *Scarface*

3. *Public Enemy*

4. *Little Caesar*

5. *Key Largo*

THE LONG ARM

Quiz A

1.
| 1. I | 2. E | 3. B | 4. H | 5. A |
| 6. J | 7. C | 8. F | 9. D | 10. G |

2.
| 1. G | 2. H | 3. B | 4. J | 5. A |
| 6. C | 7. I | 8. E | 9. F | 10. D |

3.
| 1. G | 2. I | 3. B | 4. H | 5. J |
| 6. E | 7. F | 8. A | 9. C | 10. D |

4.
| 1. J | 2. I | 3. H | 4. A | 5. B |
| 6. G | 7. E | 8. D | 9. C | 10. F |

4.
| 1. H | 2. J | 3. I | 4. A | 5. G |
| 6. C | 7. E | 8. B | 9. F | 10. D |

Quiz B

1. True. **2.** True. **3.** False. Only one officer was murdered. **4.** False. The part was played by Denver Pyle. **5.** False. He first meets Bogart in the city morgue. **6.** False. Bendix was his friend and fellow-officer; Horace McMahon was his superior. **7.** True. **8.** False. Kurt Katch played the part. **9.** False. Orson Welles played the part. **10.** True.

Quiz C

| **1.** D | **2.** B | **3.** A | **4.** B | **5.** C |
| **6.** A | **7.** B | **8.** A | **9.** A | **10.** C |

Quiz D

| **1.** B | **2.** C | **3.** E | **4.** A | **5.** D |

Quiz E

1. *Flamingo Road*

2. *The Enforcer*

3. *Across the Pacific*

4. *Notorious*

5. *The Man on the Eiffel Tower*

BAD WOMEN

Quiz A

1.	1. B	2. C	3. D	4. A	5. E
2.	1. F	2. C	3. B	4. E	5. D
	6. A				
3.	1. B	2. C	3. A	4. E	5. D
4.	1. B	2. D	3. E	4. C	5. A
5.	1. E	2. C	3. A	4. B	5. D

Quiz B

1. True.   **2.** False. Bebe Daniels played the role in 1931. Bette Davis played the part in the second movie based on the same Dashiell Hammett story, which was retitled *Satan Met a Lady*. Davis' name was also changed from Brigid O'Shaughnessy to Valerie Purvis in the second version.   **3.** True.   **4.** True.   **5.** False. It was Judith Anderson.   **6.** True.   **7.** False. Janet Leigh, her sister in the film, was the thief.   **8.** True. **9.** False. Olivia *is* Bette's cousin but the film is *Hush . . . Hush, Sweet Charlotte.*   **10.** False. The other way around; Bette was the mentally disturbed murderess.

Quiz C

1. C   **2.** A   **3.** B   **4.** C   **5.** A
6. B   **7.** B   **8.** C   **9.** A   **10.** A

Quiz D

1. C   **2.** A   **3.** B   **4.** E   **5.** D

Quiz E

1. *Bonnie and Clyde*

2. *Rebecca*

3. *Notorious*

4. *Caged*

5. *Play Misty For Me*

GUNMEN & PEACEMAKERS

Quiz A

1. 1. E   2. D   3. B   4. A   5. C
2. 1. B   2. D   3. A   4. C
3. 1. B   2. E   3. A   4. F   5. D
     6. C

4.   1. E   2. F   3. B   4. C   5. D
        6. A

5.   1. D   2. E   3. A   4. B   5. C

6.   1. C   2. A   3. B   4. E   5. D

7.   1. B   2. A   3. E   4. C   5. D

Quiz B

1. False. The other way around: Heflin plays the farmer.
2. True.   **3.** False. Valone is in the film, but it is Johnny Cash who meets Douglas in the street.   **4.** True.   **5.** True.   **6.** False. John Ireland shoots Jesse.   **7.** False. Faylen plays a crooked sheriff in the movie. Lyle Betger is Ike.   **8.** True.   **9.** True. **10.** False. Keach plays Frank James; Cole Younger is played by David Carradine.

Quiz C

1. B   **2.** A   **3.** D   **4.** B   **5.** A

6. D   **7.** B   **8.** B   **9.** A   **10.** B

Quiz D

1. D   **2.** C   **3.** E   **4.** B   **5.** A

Quiz E

1. *Hour of the Gun*

2. *High Noon*

3. *Butch Cassidy and the Sundance Kid*

4. *The Wild Bunch*

5. *True Grit*

BEHIND THE GRAY WALLS

Quiz A

1.
1. G	2. H	3. E	4. B	5. F
6. C	7. D	8. A	9. J	10. I
11. L	12. K	13. O	14. M	15. N

2.
1. B	2. O	3. N	4. C	5. M
6. L	7. D	8. E	9. A	10. F
11. G	12. H	13. K	14. J	15. I

3.
1. J	2. F	3. B	4. H	5. I
6. A	7. C	8. G	9. D	10. E

4.
1. H	2. C	3. A	4. I	5. B
6. D	7. J	8. E	9. G	10. F

5.
1. D	2. A	3. B	4. E	5. C

Quiz B

1. True. **2.** True. **3.** False. This final scene, which showed Edward G. Robinson looking through the glass panel to see MacMurray strapped to the chair in the gas chamber was cut from the film. **4.** False. Preston Foster plays the role in the 1932 movie, although Gable had made the part famous on Broadway. **5.** True. **6.** True. **7.** False. Ford was a "new fish" in the movie; Barton MacLane led the break. **8.** False. He was strapped to the front of a coal car as a shield during a break and machine-gunned to death. **9.** True. **10.** False. The inmates applaud Robert Redford as he departs.

Quiz C

1. A	2. C	3. A	4. B	5. B
6. B	7. B	8. C	9. B	10. A

Quiz D

1. B   **2.** A   **3.** E   **4.** C   **5.** D

Quiz E

1. *San Quentin*
2. *Angels with Dirty Faces*
3. *Each Dawn I Die*
4. *Birdman of Alcatraz*
5. *Brute Force*

MURDER MOST FOUL AND OTHERWISE

Quiz A

1.   1. B   2. C   3. A
2.   1. B   2. A   3. D   4. C
3.   1. B   2. C   3. E   4. D   5. A
        6. G   7. F
4.   1. D   2. A   3. E   4. B   5. C
5.   1. E   2. D   3. B   4. C   5. A
6.   1. C   2. A   3. F   4. B   5. D
        6. E
7.   1. D   2. E   3. A   4. C   5. B
8.   1. E   2. D   3. C   4. B   5. A
9.   1. C   2. A   3. D   4. E   5. B
10. 1. F   2. E   3. A   4. B   5. G
        6. D   7. C
11. 1. B   2. C   3. A   4. E   5. D

12. 1. A   2. C   3. B

13. 1. B   2. C   3. A

14. 1. A   2. B   3. C

15. 1. B   2. D   3. C   4. A

Quiz B

1. True.   **2.** True.   **3.** False. Joseph Cotton plays the role.   **4.** False. Bellamy was the psychiatrist; Chester Morris was the killer.   **5.** True.   **6.** False. Bogart gives his wives poisoned milk.   **7.** False. Webb pushes Bendix out of a skyscraper window.   **8.** False. Gwen tries to push McCrea from a church tower but falls himself.   **9.** True.   **10.** True.   **11.** True. **12.** False. Bickford, as a detective, sets out to find the murderer of Linda Darnell when he himself is the killer. **13.** False. Just the other way around.   **14.** False. The film was based upon the Leopold-Loeb case.   **15.** False. The priest is wrongly accused; O. E. Hasse, who has confessed the murder to Clift, is the real killer. **16.** True.   **17.** True.   **18.** False. Kirk Douglas is the mass killer.   **19.** False. The parts are played by McGraw and William Conrad.   **20.** True.

Quiz C

1. B   **2.** B   **3.** B   **4.** C   **5.** C

6. B   **7.** C   **8.** A   **9.** A   **10.** B

11. B   **12.** A   **13.** C   **14.** B   **15.** A

Quiz D

1. C   **2.** A   **3.** D   **4.** E   **5.** B

Quiz E

1. *Wait Until Dark*

2. *Frenzy*

3. *Monsieur Verdoux*

4. *The Treasure of the Sierra Madre*

5. *Midnight Lace*

INSIDE THE OUTFIT

Quiz A

1. 1. G   2. F   3. H   4. I   5. A
     6. J   7. B   8. C   9. D   10. E

2. 1. C   2. F   3. A   4. H   5. B
     6. J   7. D   8. I   9. G   10. E

3. 1. C   2. D   3. A   4. E   5. B

4. 1. D   2. A   3. B   4. E   5. C

5. 1. B   2. A   3. E   4. C   5. D

Quiz B

1. True.   **2.** False. Silva attempts to kill syndicate leaders in an extortion scheme.   **3.** True.   **4.** False. The lead role is played by Cameron Mitchell.
5. False. It was Sonny Corleone, played by James Caan.
6. False. It was prostitution.   **7.** True.   **8.** False. Martin Gabel plays the role.   **9.** True.   **10.** False. Talia Shire plays the sister to the Corleone thugs.

Quiz C

1. C   **2.** A, B   **3.** B   **4.** B   **5.** C

6. B   **7.** A   **8.** C   **9.** C   **10.** B

Quiz D

1. B   **2.** E   **3.** D   **4.** C   **5.** A

Quiz E

1. *The Brotherhood*

2. *Pay or Die*

3. *Godfather, Part I*

4. *Force of Evil*

5. *The Black Hand*

THE CAPER

Quiz A

1.	1. E	2. D	3. A	4. C	5. B
2.	1. D	2. A	3. B	4. E	5. C
3.	1. G	2. J	3. H	4. F	5. I
	6. A	7. D	8. B	9. C	10. E
4.	1. C	2. A	3. B	4. E	5. D
5.	1. D	2. E	3. C	4. B	5. A

Quiz B

1. False. Borgnine plans the robbery with Alan Ladd.
2. False. Faye Dunaway is the agent.   **3.** True.
4. True.   **5.** False. Peter O'Toole and others are Irish dissidents.   **6.** False. The raid is planned against Fort Knox.   **7.** True.   **8.** False. They're after a jewel-encrusted sword.   **9.** False. The film was directed by William Wyler.   **10.** True.

Quiz C

1. B	**2.** D	**3.** C	**4.** B	**5.** A. B
6. D	**7.** C	**8.** B	**9.** C	**10.** A

Quiz D

1. B	**2.** D	**3.** C	**4.** E	**5.** A

Quiz E

1. *Key Largo*
2. *The Getaway*
3. *The Asphalt Jungle*
4. *Ocean's Eleven*
5. *The Brink's Job*

MISCELLANEOUS MISCREANTS

Quiz A

1.	1. F	2. H	3. B	4. A	5. C
	6. D	7. I	8. G	9. J	10. E
2.	1. B	2. I	3. A	4. C	5. J
	6. G	7. H	8. D	9. E	10. F
3.	1. M	2. E	3. N	4. F	5. D
	6. G	7. O	8. A	9. R	10. B
	11. S	12. H	13. I	14. Q	15. P
	16. J	17. K	18. C	19. T	20. L
4.	1. B	2. C	3. D	4. E	5. A
5.	1. D	2. C	3. E	4. B	5. A

Quiz B

1. False. Vic Morrow plays the rapist.   **2.** False. Coburn is a con man in the film.   **3.** True.   **4.** True.   **5.** True.   **6.** False. Dennis O'Keefe is the newspaperman.   **7.** False. Robert Taylor plays the husband; Mitchum plays the brother of the man Taylor has killed.   **8.** False. The part is played by Steve Cochran.   **9.** False. The part is played by Humphrey Bogart, who kills Foran.   **10.** False. The guru is played by Eduardo Cianelli; Biberman plays his son.

Quiz C

1. A   **2.** B   **3.** A   **4.** C   **5.** B
6. C   **7.** A   **8.** A   **9.** C   **10.** A

Quiz D

1. B   **2.** C   **3.** A   **4.** E   **5.** D

Quiz E

1. *The Roaring Twenties*
2. *The Desperate Hours*
3. *Dark Passage*
4. *Nightmare Alley*
5. *The Night Has a Thousand Eyes*

Quiz F

1. James Cagney, Virginia Mayo and Margaret Wycherly are watching *Task Force* in the drive-in.

2. Warren Beatty, Faye Dunaway and Michael J. Pollard are watching *Gold Diggers of 1933* in the theater.

3. The convicts in the prison theater are watching *Wings of the Navy.*

4. The chain gang prisoners in the church are watching a cartoon.

Final Scoring

THE P.I.s   _____

GANGSTERS AND GUN MOLLS   _____

THE LONG ARM   _____

BAD WOMEN   _____

GUNMEN & PEACEMAKERS   _____

BEHIND THE GRAY WALLS   _____

MURDER FOUL AND OTHERWISE   _____

INSIDE THE OUTFIT   _____

THE CAPER   _____

MISCELLANEOUS MISCREANTS   _____

    Book Total Score   _____

Your Overall Rating as an Expert On Crime Movies

If your overall score is between 3,705 and 3,334   You should be running Paramount Studios, *at least.*

If your overall score is between 3,333 and 2,778   You should be head of production on all crime pictures.

If your overall score is between 2,777 and 1,852   You'll have a tough time getting by the guard at the studio gate.

MISCELLANEOUS PHOTOGRAPHS

Page vi.   TOP: Jimmy Cagney and Mae Clark in *Public Enemy.*

BOTTOM: From left: Michael J. Pollard, Faye Dunaway, and Warren Beatty in *Bonnie and Clyde.*

Page 4.   Nigel Bruce as Dr. Watson and Basil Rathbone as Sherlock Homes.

Page 22.   Joel McCrea and Humphrey Bogart in *Dead End.*

Page 40.   Steve Inhat in *Madigan.*

Page 55.   Faye Emerson in *The Mask of Dimitrios.*

Page 69.   Kirk Douglas and Elsa Martinelli in *The Indian Fighter.*

Page 84.   Victor Mature in *Kiss of Death.*

Page 100.   A scene from *Murders in the Rue Morgue.*

Page 119.   Jimmy Cagney and Humphrey Bogart in *The Roaring Twenties.*

Page 133.   A scene from *Gangs of Chicago.*

Page 147.   Humphry Bogart in *To Have and Have Not.*

Page 162.   Tony Curtis, Marilyn Monroe, and Jack Lemmon in *Some Like it Hot.*